## Praise for **THE IN-BETWEENS**

"Loeb's debut memoir crackles with light, breaking open each superb chapter to uncover a memorable and gripping origin story."

— Aimee Nezhukumatathil, author of
*World of Wonders*

"Sentence to sentence, *The In-Betweens* is awake to the awe of being in a body and the danger of negotiating a culture that wants to drive space between us, inside us. Davon Loeb is writing to stay alive under the harshest conditions, and he has given us a brilliant, devastating book."

— Paul Lisicky, author of *Later: My Life at the Edge of the World*

"Confession, manifesto, bildungsroman, and prayer, *The In-Betweens* is a meditation on bruise and healing. Loeb's struggles become snapshots of how transformation occurs even where shards have been piled, where one waits 'for something to happen, like flashes of red and blue and sirens pulsing.' A truly extraordinary new voice."

— Roy G. Guzmán, author of *Catrachos*

# THE
# IN-BETWEENS

..........

*A*
*Lyrical*
*Memoir*

..........

# DAVON LOEB

WEST VIRGINIA UNIVERSITY PRESS
MORGANTOWN

West Virginia University Press edition February 2023
Printed in the United States of America

ISBN 978-1-952271-74-8 (paperback) / 978-1-952271-75-5 (ebook)

Library of Congress Control Number: 2022948210

Cover design by Rachel Willey
Cover image courtesy of Davon Loeb
Book design by Than Saffel / WVU Press

*To all the bodies that became my memoir*
*and to my wife and children*

# CONTENTS

.........

# THE IN-BETWEENS

# A LOVE STORY

.........

SOMETIMES they played tennis together. I bet he still thinks of it often, and maybe the sun remembers it too—the way it would shine on her skin, like it was shining on her. And her skin did look best in the month of May, her birthday month, and he bought her a present to match her racket. He might surprise her on the next serve. She was rather terrible at tennis, even though she swung as if she thought she was Billie Jean King, and she was not Billie Jean King. So, he always let her win. *Match point Harry* and she'd twirl, her skirt spinning like an umbrella top. He'd hold his breath, try and capture the moment, capture her smell, capture her happiness. And even then, her perfume made flowers outside the fence pollinate and attracted bees that buzzed nearby. And Harry held his breath longer, to keep her in—maybe hold it forever if he could. She said *let's play again.* They did play, even after the other courts emptied. And after that, when the Polos and Dockers and Benzes and BMWs all drove away, he thought about what he might say, reaching into his pocket like reaching into his chest and then kneeling to give her the present.

He thought about everything that led up to that moment. He thought about when they first passed the mouth mirror and scaler, when she was just his dental hygienist, she, who was working at the dentist office while finishing nursing school and in the military. He thought about how he always held the door for her when seeing her almost a mile away in the parking lot. So what if he was late for his first appointment. So what if the secretaries suspected. So what if everyone knew. He thought about the love they had made, as if breathing for the first time, as if breathing into each other, a resuscitation of sorts. He thought about the way her irises looked when their eyelashes touched, like all the soil of Earth planted somewhere inside her eyes—how the world would ignite and felt like it might explode following that next kiss. How he didn't care if that did happen, if the world ended, as long as they were together—how it would all be worth it. She was worth it. And how on those tennis courts, he wasn't sure if he was chasing the ball or if he was chasing her.

·········

He would have finished an everything bagel with lox and passed the creamer to his wife, and she'd whisk her coffee to distract from discussing something important like bills and—also at the table—their twelve- and seven-year-old boys, who'd be excited about playing tennis sometime after school with their father. And they'd look the same, the man and boys at the table, all with light olive skin, curly hair, and faces without the strain and worry of things besides what's simple, like burnt toast. It would be a normal Monday morning before driving to the dental office.

Before arriving at work, she would have already dressed her eight-year-old daughter and three-year-old son. Braided her daughter's hair into billowy black puffs and brushed her son's hair flat, and then sent them off to school and day-care. She would love them deeply, her children, down to the marrow. They would have smelled like cocoa butter and been smooth to the touch. Their skin would be the same hue, a soft brown. She would have kissed them and then her husband, who she met sometime before while serving in the military. She'd be excited for work, wearing blue scrubs and sneakers. Her body would be young and beautiful, and her mind would be somewhere else.

It would be a weekday. It was always a weekday, and they planned it in advance, scheduling the same date off. They worked at the hospital together. He was a dentist, and she was his dental hygienist. And being together on week-days meant they wouldn't miss important time with their families; and this also meant that on weekdays, their fami-lies thought they were at work.

They wanted to avoid the adulterous clichés: lunch-break trysts, storage closets, hotel rooms, sedan back seats—for they believed and promised what they had was love and nothing less. So, they agreed it was important to be nat-ural and normal and experience life with each other as if they were really with each other. And this meant being in public—doing things, activities, not just lunches in far-out towns. They knew plenty of people who cheated, but this was different.

If they drove in his car, they listened to Beethoven and Mozart cassette tapes. With his hands, he chased the rising crescendos as if he'd composed the songs himself. He wanted to tell her the history of the songs, about the tones and shapes of the instruments. He wanted to tell her all those things that he knew, but he didn't. It might make him look older than he already looked. For they were very different, and no matter how much they loved each other, it was impossible not to notice how unalike they were. How could he not feel insecure? Listening to classical music was too appropriately matched with his grayed and receding hair. He could dye it, he thought. He could change it for her. He could wear the latest brands of clothes or buy a faster car—or do whatever else she wanted.

If they drove in her car, they listened to the latest Whitney Houston song, "I Wanna Dance with Somebody," and she would karaoke to it the best she could, strong and candid and from her diaphragm. She wasn't much of a singer. But she felt a sense of freedom with him, like driving in a convertible. She sang, and she danced and was alive. Then, the springtime air blew through the hand-cranked windows, and the smell of her lotion filled the car. And they both smiled big, taking in those rare moments of having no worries: no concerns of unpaid bills, of children, of what arguments—those typical arguments—they were going to have with their spouses when they returned later as they tiptoed around the obvious unhappiness they felt whenever saying *I love you* to someone else.

They had little in common, and their taste in music was just one example. Maybe every time an old song played, it was a reminder of just how different they were. Sometimes while listening to the radio, she'd say *my mom loves this song*, and he'd shrug it off. She'd say *I remember listening to this song as a kid*, and he'd try to pretend not to know the words to whatever the tune. But he'd remember those songs and those years when he was younger. He'd remember Sam Cooke in the '60s, James Brown, the Platters, Nat King Cole in the '50s, the Andrew Sisters, Buddy Holly, Bing Crosby in the '40s, Ella Fitzgerald, and Harry James, and he would remember the twenty-five years of living before she was even born. So how could she not think he was almost as old as her father, and how could he not think the same. It was a lifetime of difference.

From the outside, they knew not one eye would ever go unrolled, or someone's two brows would ever unfurl, because the world and everyone in it would always be watching, judging, reminding them there was nothing normal, acceptable, appropriate to this thing they called love. He was married to a woman his age and a father of two. She was married to a man her age and a mother of two. And he was white, and she Black, and this was America.

.........

On days when the weather was warm, they visited a nature center. It was quiet there, and they could barely hear the

New Jersey bustle—the cars idling, the impatient honks, the thick pollutant that sounded like water in the ear. It was their retreat, and nature blanketed them from everything outside the over two hundred acres of wilderness. Though people still stared and side-eyed. They mumbled things and said what they wanted to; but whatever those people said, some white and some Black, they didn't care much, for they swore the sun shined just on them, as if one of those crepuscular rays from God. They said the whole thing was destiny and never mind what other people thought. In a way, they related to the nature conservatory, this beautiful thing just being miles away from the city and yet tucked away from the busy Tri-State. It was as if being in two different places at the same time. And this was often how they felt, while eating dinner or washing dishes at their homes, while in their beds with their spouses, while living every moment away from each other, as if lying, every day, under oath, an oath that said *you are white, you are Black, you are married, your love is very wrong.*

But at the nature center, they could see the Hudson River from different markers on the trails. They would stop, watch the waters travel, and talk of the future. They made plans. They agreed on who would leave whom first, where they would live, that her children would take his name—maybe a big wedding or just something small at the county office. What dreams they had, to run away and start fresh and new. Everything would be better. And then, even the Hudson seemed to smell like an ocean, and the water's surface was clearer, bluer; and above that, the countless hemlocks stretched like giant paint strokes of different shades of green; and above that, two birds, like my mother and father, flocked together, and they too, dreamt of migrating.

# ON I-85 SOUTH

.........

THE exterior was like the car had just driven through a sandstorm: rusted, chipped paint, exposed primer. There was one tire of a different size that replaced an original, so it wobbled on its axis. And you'd have to lick your fingers and twist a couple wires for the radio to work, the voices cutting on and off, from FM to AM to silence. The car needed struts. The car needed pads. The car needed blades for its wipers that etched semicircles in the glass. And something black and tarry and thick that was reminiscent of motor oil dripped and had been following us from our departure. But it ran, like how a smoker with emphysema ran. And you might not have been able to tell who was more broken—the car or her—how her hair had split ends and was wrapped in something faded and frilly, and the frames she usually only wore before bed magnified hot and puffy dark eyes, and she had pulled on whatever sweatpants and sweatshirt she could find in the closet, so her clothes didn't match, her perfume wasn't sprayed, and she might not have showered at all. And while this does not define a broken woman, this woman was in pieces.

Like this car, the two-door 1984 Chevette with no frills—no automated windows, no cassette tape player, no leather seats, no air conditioner—just a box on wheels with an engine. And it sputtered, hissed, and wheezed. When she continued forgetting to press the clutch, the gears ground, and we covered our ears, and the metal on metal sounded like two cars, like two pulleys, pushing into each other. Like us, crammed together in the back seat, my big sister and big brother and me, a trio of nesting dolls. We watched our mother become something else. For on a normal day, before all of this happened, before the rage and panic, she was regal: double-breasted blazer, pleated pants, blouses begonia-bright and feathery-petal soft. Our mother was planned, precise, purposeful, like the inside of a paper planner. But now, she said things under her upheaving chest, the rising and falling of breath as if she were still pacing around our house, still throwing whatever she could into her military-issued duffel: a sleeve of diapers, a pack of wipes, a set of Nancy Drews, a brigade of army men, a photo album, a manila envelope, handfuls of clothes, and snacks in baggies.

This was after her divorce, but before she signed the papers, just when she left—when she'd had enough. The lies had grown like a cancer grows and had spread from her heart throughout her body and her home—how the lies were in the walls, how they were asbestos, how their home was poison, how the foundation had been eaten away, how it was not safe, how she couldn't take it a moment more.

While driving for however long on I-95, she imagined herself as a frontier woman in her caravan with her children—that when she stepped on the gas it was like horses galloping on a dirt road, and that the billow of smoke was just the dust of tumbleweeds, and that the sun looked new now, an orange she'd never seen before, as if the insides of a grapefruit, and she thought it was the same sun some woman had seen when she moved westward, and that woman didn't need a husband either, that she could load the wagon, that she was strong, and she was a fit mother, and that between third and fourth gear, this mother, our mother, secured her left hand to the steering wheel, and her right hand unfolded a map across the passenger seat, and her finger followed a route on that map that she had traced in red marker the night before. And on that highway, living a day in that car, as if following some emergency broadcast, we just had to drive—drive like we were runaways.

# MY MOTHER'S MOTHER

.........

BUT when I imagine my mother's mother, all I can see is her tying an apron around her waist, and there is a dark smudge in the middle, like how some old white crowds stood watching the swinging knot around someone's neck that my mother's mother knew. And yet, still, she soaked her hands—wrinkled and wet—the brined black leather in the blinking soapsuds, washing china and other plates from other places she would never go. And so what if she lumbered, and she stretched, and she cleaned, and she wiped her tired brow because her shackled wrists could earn only enough change for the back seat ride on the bus home?

And while cleaning those houses, polishing wood and dusting corners, she and the many other Black women she knew reminisced about some old promises. Someone long ago said that they'd all get a mule and forty acres. And the promise lingered—the notion that one day things would be better, that they'd finally have a leg up, start fresh, start new—endless possibilities. And this even motivated some of those women to scrub harder, dig deep into their souls, but my mother's mother would say *you're promised nothing but your first name.* Maybe she was a pessimist, or maybe she just really considered things, like lineage. She considered how they used to be slaves, all of them, with no savings accounts, no trust funds, no land, no family money. Rather, they were unshackled in 1865, and kicked in the ass, *get*, their masters said.

And they got going, with some scraps of skin still on their backs. Then again, that's just one chapter in the story, one narrative that belongs to a part of her but not all of her. It's important for me to tell you that her life is not to be defined by all that struggle. There was beauty in her body and skin before it was bent and broken and blackened—her skin was just skin before. And maybe there's irony in all of this, thinking back on her childhood, the whole southern home, her living life normally: breakfast at seven, lemonade, Sunday school, and the way love smelled like butter and bread around a dinner table. I'm so ashamed by how surprised that makes me feel. How hard it is to imagine her as my mother's mother first and her color second. How it's so much quicker to assume what it meant to be her was what it meant to be Black, and nothing else—with no separation. Maybe it's instinctual to take on her narrative and tell you those prerequisite hardships: about inequality, discrimination, and what it might have meant to be Black back then. But to be honest, I don't know; she never told me. I just know her name, and her face, and the way she could tell me the past as if it were yesterday.

.........

She was born in 1932. One of eight children—five brothers and three sisters. From a big family, but also from a *bigger family, God's family*, my mother's mother would say. So, when one of those sisters died as a baby, they knew it wasn't the end; they knew God had just brought her home sooner rather than later. They buried that little baby somewhere out on their farm, and on the third day, the sun said *rise*, and flowers grew from out that grave: lilies and mayapples. *It was a miracle*, some proclaimed, and everyone believed it. Because back then, on any given Sunday, you could see optimism alive on those mornings—alive in the sun, alive in their eyes, how it was all the same. And they hummed the old hymns together, hands held, like a ladder, strong and bound and candid, while walking to church. Nothing could stop them, not rains, nor winds, nor any weather, because Sunday, family, and God was rightfully theirs—if nothing else was in America.

Even though they barely owned their own name, they did own a house, somewhere in rural Coy, Alabama. And no matter how bad things were for Black people in America, my mother's mother would say *we still had our pride*. She'd say *no matter if they told us we could drink from this but couldn't drink from that, if we could sit there but not here, go to that school and not this one, we still had that house.* She said this with pride because ownership is undefined by race, because blood and sweat, no matter if one were Black or white, would always be the same color. And that house that her family owned, her daddy built from the ground up. It was beautiful by any standard. For he built it with callus and hammer, with muscle and brawn, and as she said *with God in his belly, pushing his body, strengthening his heart, board by board, stretching from floor to wall to roof, an altar to his family.* My mother's mother would say that maybe some things were built better back then, things like family.

They owned that house outright but did not own the 160 acres of farmland. It was leased land. And the real owners said my mother's mother and her family could stay there as long as they wanted, forever and a day, but the land would never be theirs, for their skin would never change. They could build there, start their lives, marry, give birth, and die, but never, in any deed would it say *this land is your land.* And in Coy, her family was one of the only Black families to actually own a home—to actually say *this is ours.*

Some people they knew, other lots from church, side-eyed, whispered about her family going back home to *The Big House, where them white people let them stay.* And even white families across the street, coming out of their church, looked with envy in their eyes, knowing they were trotting back to a little shack. But my mother's mother and her family walked out of the church service with their heads high, in their Sunday best: elaborate prim pillbox hats, skinny ties, two-toned Oxfords, dresses like giant flowers, and their Bibles at their sides, shielding them from whatever wasn't God's will. And somebody, white or Black, probably said that they looked so much different than how they first arrived in the South.

. . . . . . . . .

The land surrounding the house was covered by hundreds of trees—thick, swollen, sturdy trees, trees that never warped under the hulking Alabama sun, trees whose boughs never broke, trees whose roots never loosened, trees that lived for however many years in testament to never change. They were imposing and often frightened my mother's mother. As a child, she swore they watched her. She said there were crows in some; crows that crowded the branches and cawed viciously. And in other trees, when the wind blew, she thought she heard the willows lean in and whisper to each other, maybe saying *we're finin' get ya*. And how some of the biggest trees, the ones that reached the far ends of the property, stood heavy and lopsided—as if still holding the weight of something—and that those were the trees her daddy told her about, told my mother's mother what those trees were really for.

# BATH TIME

.........

SOMETIMES when the hot water was cut off, my big sister
boiled large pots of water in the kitchen. She'd turn down
the eye of the electric stove and cautiously lift the brimming pot with two dishrags. I'd stand next to her, her little
brother, trailing her shadow, and walk the whole way with
her to the bathroom. It reminded me so much of Sunday
mornings when my sister pulled her two little brothers
from our beds. Wrapped in sheets, we were little ghosts,
booing all the way to the bathroom, where my brother and
I shouldered for the sink and brushed for three minutes because our sister always counted. And then the tag-behind,
fitting our feet in the wet divot of her arch like a family of
baby ducks—one and one and one, together.

While the water steamed, my sister looked away and
briefly down at me, and she could be like our mother, like
when she dressed me for church—tied my bite-sized oxfords
and clipped on my tie—and how I loved her then, loved her
even when her side-ponytail turned to fire—the hair oil and
brimstone, and how it set my world aflame—or the one

look, the one sharp furling glare that turned me to stone and snakes hissed all over her head—and the Silent Treatments, the tickle torments, the untransformed Transformers—and the things I stole: her troll dolls, cassette tapes, scrunchies, earrings, and everything else that looked fun and foreign. Even then, I knew my sister would still carry those boiling pots that were always brimming over.

In the bathroom, she said the water will cool off fast, and I looked at her like I would never forget what that dependency felt like. She started pouring the water into the bath and maybe this time the water was too hot, or the bath was already too full, but whatever it was, hot water splashed everywhere. My sister pushed me and dropped the pot, and it emptied, and the water was red, and her body screamed in the way only our bodies could react to shock—guttural, uncontrollable, a loss of language. When she tried to unpeel her pink corduroy pants, the thick cotton was lined with her skin.

Sometimes I think that the only real thing we can ever offer each other are our bodies.

# THE RECONSTRUCTION
# OF A SLAVE

.........

MY great-great-grandfather was a slave. The story goes
that he wouldn't walk—and couldn't walk—so he never
left the bed, which was probably just a gnarl of rags on
the floor with his body tangled, deadened, saturated, and
cooking like meat waiting to be salted, cooked by a sun so
hot it could peel back skin as sharp as it could warp wood.
Nana said that one day, along the grapevines of planta-
tions, word of freedom was sprouting. This could have been
a year or a day before actual slavery abolition—but words
are fire and flint is rumor, and I bet even the mosquitoes
profiting off the Black bodies felt the heavy stickiness in the
air. *Lord knows*, Nana would say, *black skin ain't what it
used'ta*. And in some way, I knew what she meant: I could
see Great-great-grandfather's belly breathe into himself in
a constant panic, the anxiety like a suffocation, waiting for
the wilts to settle, the throbbing warmth of scars reopen-
ing like soil with garden prongs. Great-great-grandfather's

ankles barely visible as hands reached and grabbed, like long branches dragging the smudge of a boy facedown through the dirt.

Nana said Great-great-grandfather was no fool, as young as he was. No one knew why he couldn't walk. Maybe something like how only the Lord knows why this baby was born with broken legs the way they are. Legend writes itself to ear and mind and hope, and Great-great-grandfather became a salvation like Christ in the upper pews where Blacks worshipped for some chance that someone would rise up and walk them to freedom. It all reminds me so much of the Baptist churches Nana brought me to, bodies swaying the way trees swayed, and hands like the thunderclaps of summer heat storms, a unison of sorts. The whole thing entranced me, like the crescendos of accepting Christ and hallelujahs as the Holy Spirit enters you. And maybe these tributaries to Christ kept Great-great-grandfather alive—as he was propped up, and something like a bowl was tilted and his throat retched a little until whatever was soaking in the discolored thing drained like sewage into his stomach—and hands held and heads fell, and thank God for this food.

Those who remembered something of their old gods and lands and rituals might have sung a song that even he couldn't understand, and I can't comprehend; but whatever it was, it may have been the only assurance a slave could hold on to. And Great-great-grandfather for ten years as a child did not walk, and some say it was his refusal to be a slave—they say, heroically, Great-great-grandfather chose not to walk and therefore could not slave in the fields, and

the bolls of cotton that waited to be picked from the billowy whiteness burnt that day, and the pruned backs that
blocked the sun stretched out their wrinkles and began
elsewhere. And then Great-great-grandfather wiggled his
charcoaled toes, and heavy-hand planted his palms, and
rooted his heels deep into the dirt floor, and rose up—his
knees knobby, thinned, and grayed—and I bet before it
all, they all said *praise Jesus*, and Great-great-grandfather
stood erect and walked away as a free man.

# AT CHURCH

.........

On Sundays, we dragged our feet, wishing we were still in bed—rubbing our rheumy eyes and bellies that were growling for breakfast. We ate cereal, only a splash of milk each. We elbowed for space to sit, two in a chair, cursing at each other. We raved about how boring church would be, and how we'd rather be here, out front in the grass or in the street, playing some game of chase or catch in the Alabama summer sunlight. But Nana demanded our attendance. And while we ate, she'd get ready in her Sunday dress, the one she laid out the night before, something floral, iron-pressed, and sprayed with her favorite perfume. She sang in the choir and needed to be early. So, she'd delegate the oldest of us to get everyone else ready.

We'd huddle around the single bathroom vanity—wash-cloths and soap in the armpits, gurgling and passing the mouthwash, brushing with the toughest bristle brush through crinkled hair, and wash the spit from around our dry mouths. We knew we had to look our best because God would be watching.

This church wasn't the same church Nana went to as a child, but it was the same God. And though Nana's body changed—aged, rounded—her voice hoarse, raspy, her eyes were still the same, still that earthy brown that brimmed with the vitality of soil.

Before service started, we could hear her as we walked through the big red entrance doors. Her voice and the voices of other choir-women and organ keys reverberated and filled the entire nave, giving it the impression of being a bigger room. In retrospect, the church was small and quaint, maybe fitting fifty people; though back then, everything was large from our perspective. The church was imposing—the sharp steeple, the crucifixes, the depictions of Jesus on calvary, the preacher with the baritone voice that sounded as God would sound, all of it. And after we trickled in, our feet still heavy, one by one, wrinkled shirts, ties, and dresses, following the oldest of us, we'd settle in the pews, tightly—hips and butts on top and touching.

The big sturdy man in the purple gown was a monument at the altar. His body and his sermon taking on some kind of violence—how he slammed his brick-sized hands on the pulpit, how his voice carried, the cadence changing as if manic—telling his parish stories about pain, about grace. I remember learning about a man named Job, whose affliction was unimaginable. I remember the preacher recited the tale without one glance into his Bible. I remember how Job lost everything, how his children died, how his body was sickened, how his wealth was taken—and all the while, Job never denounced God—how Job loved God, even then, loved Him more than ever. Silent for a moment, and then the preacher leaned on the podium, the bulk of the man causing the wood to creak loudly—but in almost a whisper, he said: *Faith, Job had faith.*

But what I remember more are the pews being uncomfortably hard, unwelcoming wood that made sitting feel like sitting there for hours. I remember squirming like trying to find an itch. I remember wanting to draw in the Bibles, just for something to do. I remember watching Nana in the sanctuary with the choir, swaying and singing, like those days when she was a child and church never ended. She was unlike herself, normally reserved and soft, but now, stomping, yelling, shaking—her voice becoming her body, her body inching closer to God. It was as if she took on those proverbs, as if those stories were her stories—about David and Isaiah and the Lord. And while entranced in the gospels, the claps, the stained-glass color prisms, and the rhythm of feet like some holy drums, her grandchildren, in our seats, heckled and teased Nana, nudging and whispering *listen to Nana singing; she sounds so bad, cover y'all's ears*, and I remember the way none of us really appreciated God's attention.

# LIKE GLADIATORS

.........

DURING those hot summer days in Alabama, we all sat around, dehydrated with cottonmouth and dried skin that was gray and ashen, and our bodies were hot and sticky, like being in a summer camp—bunked and communal and almost eating off each other's knobby knees, our backs hunched, biting into fried chicken and sucking the oil-plaster from under our cuticles, gnawing and spitting out marrow, and drinking red sugar water from plastic cups. Even Nana's house seemed to sweat, like meat and its fat, like a gelatin covering the skin of the walls, and the tuft of the carpet, and the upholstery around the armchairs. On a white couch covered in plastic, our bodies sounded like rubber, the moisture of an underarm or the grease of the back of the neck. And the silhouette stains we left, children cooling on the kitchen floor like making snow angels.

We played the games children often played: hide-and-seek, tag, cowboys and Indians. When hiding and seeking, we were rodents, scurrying around, fitting our bodies in the tightest of places, under the crawl space of Nana's house and below the workings of the broken-down Buick in the driveway. And when tagging, we ran circles around the cul-de-sac, screaming and gasping, our feet hot and burning, the soles of our shoes wearing down, the bunny-ear laces flopping, and Rorschach patterns of sweat stained our shirts. And the imaginary shootouts, John Wayne versus a tribe of Native Americans, when we made pistols out of our hands and bows and arrows out of our crescent-shaped arms, and how we died slow after being hit with the six-shooter. And then the rusty coloring around knee scrapes and elbow burns and split lips, and what it was like trying to wrestle the sun.

But eventually boredom arrived. What would we do after everyone was caught, and after all the Native Americans were shot, and all our shirts had been yanked, stretched, and tagged—what were we to do then? We were only allowed inside during the day for lunch, bathroom, or emergencies. Playing inside seemed forbidden. The old house couldn't take that much commotion. If we ran one loop from the guest bedroom, through the living room, and into the kitchen, the house shook. We felt it.

When Nana called us in for lunch, the floorboards creaked under the heavy bustle of our hungry feet. And when it rained or the heat index was too high and we had to come inside, we became prisoners with nothing to do: no Nintendo or Sega Genesis, no television because the adults commandeered the two cable boxes, and even the board games were unplayable for all the game pieces were missing. So, the inevitable happened when children were bored and lost interest and found things much better and more exciting to do.

We'd lick the top of nine-volt batteries, standing in a circle and watching whoever's turn it was to complete the dare, chanting *do it* with thrill and anxiety, waiting to see what would happen. The older of us went first and dramatized what would be an electric shock: shaking, eyes rolling back, falling to the floor. The younger of us, including myself, would be even more frightened, just as they intended, thinking that would happen to us. So, like dominoes, after snaking our little tongues on the metallic terminal, each person who licked the battery behaved the same way. It tasted like iron and stung like an ant bite.

We dared each other to do plenty of stupid things: eating bugs, swallowing pennies, chasing cars—a litany of nonsense with no real reason besides the boredom itself. And before making whatever poor decision, the occurrence of why was never in question. We had to do it. So much of our childhood was contractual: you did *this* and *this* happened, you did not do *that* and *that* happened. It seemed relatively simple. Those who were older had the privilege to be leaders because age meant jurisdiction. And those who were the youngest, like me, were powerless and followed without question. So, if we were told to eat a worm, we'd slurp that worm like spaghetti. The hierarchy was law, and if we broke it and told an adult, the shock of the battery was nothing compared to the consequence of being ostracized by the rest of the group.

.........

On whatever day it was, the boredom set in, and we were sitting somewhere in the grass soaking in the sun, and our skin was roasting like the way meat does when it's dried out for a couple days. With nothing else to do, one of my older cousins stood on the hood of the broken-down Buick in the driveway to gather our attention. The overcast of their body, two feet squared on the Buick's paint-chipped hood, pointed and directed and proclaimed today would be a main event and then palmed a fist into the other hand.

There were many unwritten rules of engagement: no biting, no slapping, no eye poking, no hits to the groin, and of course, no telling adults. We all knew this. Fighting was not uncommon among us. It was a rite of passage. We all fought or would fight each other at some point to prove dominance, one-on-one, and the rest of us watched or were delegated to break it up if it was too violent. Whoever was fighting would be evenly matched, about the same age and size. Altogether, Nana had fifteen grandchildren, so there would always be an opponent.

Except I had never been in a fight. I was the epitome of unathletic, all eighty pounds of me: bony, no muscle tone, wiry glasses, and a high-pitched voice to match my scrawny body. No one wanted to fight me, not even for the sheer amusement.

.........

There were eight of us enclosed in a semicircle waiting to see which two would be chosen. Our crowd became impatient, *who's fightin'*, like a whisper-down-the-lane game. The body on the car, who gathered our attention, seemed to eclipse the sun, and for a moment, darkness cast, and what words were about to be said felt foreboding, like some god coming down to tell us our future. My cousin stood on that hood and pointed at each of us: *Eeny meeny miny mo'. Catch a tiger by the toe. If he hollers, let him go. Eeny. Meeny. Miny. Mo'.* The finger landed on me, and then my cousin, a girl.

We were the same size. These two skinny things, thin as twines on noose knots and bird-chested and dwarfed under the crowd that roared and cheered and surrounded us. Our shadows silhouetted as if off gallows. And then someone stepped behind her and squeezed her wrists and mimicked punches—swinging the peg-like things forward and back. And someone came behind me and told me to square my shoulders and puff my chest and said *you better not lose to a girl.*

Immediately, her fists fired, and my lip split, and there was blood from the band of hand bones and clip-on keratin nails, and the bobbing of her hair ties like clacker toys clanging, the pink plastic balls swinging as she swung. Someone said *hit her, hit her,* and all those notions like right and wrong, and good and bad and everything else that seemed important, became nothing as loud as the humiliation. For if I hit a girl, I hit a girl, and I was never supposed to hit a girl—not even when the sun got too big for the sky and touched down on earth and burned the white right out of our teeth.

.........

Little humans are like hair cells of the inner ear when struck, cochlear nerves rattle, fluid drums, and a head becomes heads and motions and inertias and gravities, and their laughter like an echo, and the cries of a boy some twenty-five years ago, when I curled my fingers into a ball and swung them back as hard as I could, and then the painful tangibility of it all, humankind failing the way it did— the way it always does when bodies are just spectacles. And the music we made—the grit and grind of knuckles and chin and cheek—and the way they watched, with no horror, with no remorse, only applause.

# DRINKING A COLT 45

.........

MY grandfather quit cutting the grass, and the grass stuck to the resin on his hands. He pulled at his pants and adjusted the waist, and he said something about the sun doing a better job singeing than the blunt mower blades did cutting. He walked over to the garage and stood momentarily in the sun. Sweat filled his dark face, and the discolored water moved like streams in the cracks and ridges of his furrowed skin. It gave him an oily finish, and he used a once-white washcloth to wipe his forehead. Then he reached into a blue cooler. The ice shuffled as his big swollen hand wrestled with something. He pulled out a Colt 45 beer can and drove his thick thumb into the push tab—*pop*—and foam frothed. Quickly, he suctioned onto the mouth as if oxygen. He said nothing. His large fingers wrapped around the aluminum can easily like a hand-fitted tool. Mosquitoes flew around him, slow and heavy, drunk off blood. After he finished a beer, which didn't take very long, he squeezed the can, and it effortlessly collapsed into a scrappy-looking bow tie. He tossed it in a bin. Soon he had a collection.

I watched from behind the broken-down Buick on the edge of the driveway, squatting close to the ground near the big slick shadow that stained the asphalt underneath the Buick's belly pan. I was silent too, watching him and watching little bugs carry dirt from either side of the grass. The hot air pushed my glasses down, and I pushed them back up. My face still hurt. Earlier that day, my cousin and I fought—for whatever reason—and I lost. I was pinned down and punched twice in the face. My lip was swollen, and my right eye bruised. Thankfully, my thick glasses covered the soon-to-be black eye. I was happy it was hidden. I didn't want Nana to know, which would break one of those essential rules in childhood: tattling. If I told, I'd be tormented more—hell, I was already on the bottom rung. And while everyone else sat inside for lunch and played a card game, I was alone. I thought *who cares if no one wants to play with me.*

Unlike me, one of the weakest and smallest among Nana's grandchildren, my grandfather was tough, his hands leathered, knuckles callused; and even though his belly was round and distended, his shoulders were broad and muscular like a silverback gorilla. Maybe fighting was a rite of passage, something all men faced. I was sure that my grandfather had been in many brawls. It was as if he had earned some eternal confidence, a swagger and bravado about him that said *I don't take shit from nobody.*

*Get from that car, boy*, my grandfather barked. I guess

he could see all eighty pounds of me hanging near the
bumper. I did as I was told. His voice, harsh, like the way
the Buick might have sounded if it started up. He continued *boy, come here. What ya hiding there for.* His questions were statements. I snuck from around the car and
walked over to him. He was smoking a cigarette. I tried
not to cough and watched him intently—the amber glow-
ing red, the ash lengthening, the way he didn't take the cigarette out of his mouth, just perched it there, talking like
Popeye the Sailor Man. ·

I gave him my attention and readjusted my glasses, so I
could hide my purpling eye. My grandfather said *you got a
shiner, huh? Let ya grandfather see.* I took my glasses off
but kept my head down. My grandfather palmed my chin,
*look up, boy*, and he tapped my head. He inspected my
face. I was waist-high to him. He nodded, and the cigarette
nodded too. *I hope he looks worse than you*, my grandfather said, and then he chuckled, sounding exactly how an
old man would.

My grandfather balled his fist and jabbed in my direction. I flinched. He said *let me show ya.* He told me to hold
my hands open like oven mitts. Each time his giant fist, like
a boulder, struck my tiny hand, it clapped. With his mouth
half closed, he said *not bad for an old man.* I agreed and
was amazed at how well both of his fists struck with precision, completely ambidextrous, much better than how I
ever punched. Little clouds of smoke followed his movements. He said *you try.* I was hesitant but excited to imi-
tate what I saw. I swung with my right hand; my glasses
wobbled a bit. *Harder*, he said. So, I did. *Put some hip in*

*it, boy.* So I did. This went on for a couple minutes. When winded, he rested his hands and walked farther into the garage. He came back with a two-gallon bucket. He flipped it over and then let me sit awhile.

·········

The sun was lazier. Instead of being particular to where it drew, the sun spread itself in all directions. And it was pliable, fitting in anywhere like liquid. My glasses kept fogging, and I scrubbed the lenses with my shirt. My lips and throat were dry. I hadn't realized how thirsty I was. *Alabama is hotter than hell*, he smiled, his teeth yellowed and rusted. I thought it had been an hour or so since I last had something to drink. Now, in the scorching heat, my head throbbed. I could go inside, but I didn't want to leave the garage. I felt privileged to be in his company. It was rare because in our family, adults stuck with adults, kids with kids. A rule of sorts.

He drank four beers and was working on his fifth when Nana called for him to come inside for something. He hesitated. *Solomon*, she called again. He put his beer down by the cooler and the cigarette he was smoking and then walked inside, irritated. Maybe it was the heat, or the thirst, or that my grandfather wasn't there, or that maybe it was my chance to be like an adult, be a man for a moment. And then I could tell my cousins what happened, and they'd be jealous. I knew not to steal a puff of the cigarette. Hell, it was way too hot, and I'd smell like smoke and smoking killed—this I knew; but a beer wouldn't kill me. And my breath wouldn't smell if I drank only a couple sips. I stared at my grandfather's beer, and its condensation left a circle around the can, and then the circle widened, and another circle formed. I didn't have much time. He would be back soon.

It was all short-lived. I could barely swallow the beer. Retching, the bitter and foreign flavor caused me to gag. It did cool me off though. But seconds later, I coughed and spit more up. And still, my grandfather hadn't returned. Craning my neck, I searched around the garage, just to make sure. I held the cold beer with two hot hands and took another sip. Shortly after, when my grandfather returned, he picked up his beer, and I knew it was lighter than he expected. He shook the can, and it rattled. And then he peered at me, while I sat still and quietly on the bucket—not even fazed by the heat or my black eye or my grandfather's glare, the heavy muscular eyes.

# THROW THE FOOTBALL

.........

MY uncle called me a bad word when he found me playing with my cousin's dolls, and I didn't know what the word meant except it seemed not good, and I just liked playing make-believe like I did with my action figures, who were men and not women, but what did it really matter besides maybe the voices I put on when they talked? He told me to go pass a football outside with his son, but whenever I threw a football, it never spiraled; it wobbled like an egg. And maybe because I was so much better at drawing and imagining and writing and no good at running and catching and throwing, maybe I was that bad word, I thought—maybe the boy I was wasn't the type of boy I should be. That when he said it, he meant *something is very wrong with you*. So, I put the dolls down, the two Barbies with long brown hair and bright pink floral dresses, who were previously chatting about Spider-Man defeating Dr. Octopus, and then placed them back in the open-face dollhouse that had little rooms with miniature teacups and a tiny stove—one Barbie, somewhat standing by the stove, and the other sitting with her legs extended on the sofa. My uncle waited impatiently, a shadow above—and how close his body loomed because if I didn't put those dolls away, I think he was going to do something.

# A ROLL OF DUCT TAPE

.........

I'm not too sure whose idea it was, but I know it was not mine. I was strictly a follower and not a leader, blame omitted. I would have loved to have said no, suggested a lesser punishment for my girl cousin for whatever she did or did not do. But if I had, it would have been me up there, taped to that tree. Not this time though—this time I would point and laugh and not be laughed at. This was a rarity, and the harassment could easily flip. Not long ago, that very same cousin who was enticing me to help drag my girl cousin to the tree out front was the same one who locked me in a coat closet up on the top shelf. It was his way of ridding me of my fear of the dark, so he said. *Don't be a baby. Be a man. Man up.* And he tossed me around his neck, laid me out like a duffle bag. Though I did put up the mightiest fight—kicked, bit, punched, slapped, my limbs, the wings of a plucked chicken. This was Exposure Therapy: face your fears. And he pulled open the door and reached deep into the darkness and offered me to it. The coats rumbled, almost off their hangers, as if hungry gods at an altar.

But now it was her turn to be sacrificed. Fidgeting and resisting, yelling and spitting, we held her still, six hands working like lattice. We gripped her knobby body, dragging her by wrists and feet out the front door and into the backyard. We hauled her to the tree that stood like a giant arm of a mighty beast from out the ground. The three of us, wrapping the tape in circles, snarled and laughed like children *ringing around a rosy*. We bound her around her ankles with a roll of duct tape. However many circles we made, the tape was endless, giving more of itself, the backing ripping as if pulling off a scab. After she was secured, the tallest of us, the oldest, the one who we followed to hell and back, tore the final piece of tape and stuck it over her mouth. I was glad it wasn't me taped to the tree. I was glad to be on the other end of the joke.

Maybe there was no real reason why we did it. Even if there was, that was still no reason why to do it. I could say it was kids being kids, but it wasn't. I could say that I am sorry now, but I'm not. Though I can say that this was how we loved each other. So, when it started to rain, we left her there.

# SUMMER THUNDERSTORMS

.........

I hated the humidity, the way it always felt like breathing through a wet shirt. On some days, it could strangle us, the sun bloated, and the hot air was heavy like being inside of a mouth. Every droplet was salted from the bodies of the day and steam and stench lingered in the dirt. While our bodies involuntarily sweat, the heat became hotter and hotter and thicker and wetter and stickier. On days like that, the heat couldn't take it either—like it, too, needed to cool off. With nowhere to hide, it'd reach far into the clouds, and it would rain. And when it did, the streets emptied—no hollering kids, no idling cars, no bouncing balls, and the dogs stopped barking. An eerie silence about it, like God pressed pause and was going to tell us something—maybe a warning, maybe a sign, or maybe He'd say *go inside*.

We spent more than half the day outside, running circles, passing balls, playing tag, or just plain nothing. At least if it rained, we'd be allowed in. So when we did come in, we stockpiled into one room and took turns putting our faces in front of an oscillating fan. We mocked propeller noises through the dusty plastic blades if only for moments of cool relief. We snuck ice cubes from ice trays and massaged them on our hot faces, and the ice cubes melted and ran dirty. We pulled washcloths from the washroom and drenched them with cold water, and we rested them on our seared necks. But when the summer storms rolled in—as they always did—when the heat was unbearable, everyone scattered around the house and looked for a place to hide.

Though, not me—I loved the summer thunderstorms. I didn't retreat into the bedrooms or bathrooms. Instead, I watched the storm, my face pressed against the cold glass of the living room window, as the storm grew darker, the quick feeling of coolness and warmth came together like a soothing rush that made my hair rise. And outside was the same soothing rush, though moments ago the sky was brightly painted as if with a palette of flowers.

But now the sky billowed, a violent purple like skin beginning to bruise. Everything was turning inside out. And the wind couldn't catch itself, blowing in big weeping gusts, and then tight asthmatic coughs. One tree in the front yard felt the brunt of the force, the branches stiffening, tensing, a muscle. I thought I could hear it groan under the weight of the tumbling sky. I thought *what if the tree gave way, let go of its roots*. I could imagine it piece by piece, shredding like a barn in a tornado. I ducked my head under the window frame for a second.

I noticed the smudge I left on the window and wiped it with my shirt. I could see the rain starting, small droplets at first, leaving blots on the cement stoop. Within seconds, the rain poured like a faucet without a hose. And even though the window was closed, the caulk around it became wet. I could feel the rain spritzing my forearms. I knew what was coming. Wide-eyed, I counted five Mississippis. And when the thunder roared, I tried to keep my eyes open. The window shook, and so did my eyelashes. And then lightning struck in a web from the underbelly of a giant cloud. It made me feel small and fragile—homes, cars, street signs, us—it could all go in moments. And there was nothing I would have loved more than to see everything be torn apart.

# AUNT SAMMY

.........

I really liked Aunt Sammy. She laughed at everything and would tell me the kind of jokes Mom never told. When she would, she looked cool, a cigarette in her mouth bobbing as she talked. And though I was always excited to go to Aunt Sammy's, I knew Mom wouldn't like it. She left us with Nana for the summer. She told Nana not to let us go to Aunt Sammy's without Nana staying the whole time. Mom said something about how Aunt Sammy didn't really watch us kids—how *Sammy is a drunk*.

When we got there, Aunt Sammy pulled two cups from the dish rack and ran the sink water. She filled the cups, and then shuffled to a kitchen cabinet and returned with a tub of Kool-Aid. Barely reaching over the fold-out kitchen table, I watched, my eyes floated above water. *Can I try*, I asked. Without hesitation, she handed me the big wooden spoon. I dipped it in the red Kool-Aid. I pulled it out carefully, the divot brimmed with sugar, and I dropped it into the cups of water. I whisked with the spoon, spinning little red cyclones. At my house, Mom regulated how many sugary drinks we could have, but not Aunt Sammy. She didn't mind one bit. And I felt the thrill of doing something bad—Kool-Aid, like a child's liquor, normal if controlled in one or two small cups, but too much and I'd become an animal.

I sat at the table with her, drinking my Kool-Aid while she drank something dark from her cup. I could smell it, though I didn't recognize the smell. She sipped her cup, and I swigged what was left of mine.

.........

From an early age, Mom warned my brother and me of the dangers of drinking alcohol. Mom said when she was young, Aunt Sammy sometimes wouldn't return home for days. She'd be off on one of her drinking binges, and eventually she'd return home staggering like she was walking in someone else's shadow. Aunt Sammy would rave, curse, and boast about her wild nights. Mom said that wasn't the sister she knew, that *Aunt Sammy was my protector.* Mom told us how the two of them, with hands held, would cross busy streets together, that every day, Aunt Sammy walked Mom to school, for *she was an honorable big sister, a big sister anyone would want.* Though on one occasion, Aunt Sammy didn't walk Mom to school and, on that day, a group of girls who had been waiting for the right opportunity found it and harassed Mom—stepped on her shoes, tore her shirt, punched her breathless. By the very next day, Aunt Sammy found those girls, as if a bounty on their heads, and beat

them black-and-blue. Aunt Sammy was hard, Mom said, but
her heart was soft.

.........

Aunt Sammy was somewhere we—my brother, Aunt
Sammy's son Ernie, and me—were not. I was there physically but more like a shadow, undersized and almost unno-
ticeable, tagging behind as the quintessential little brother.
I was all hopped up on Kool-Aid, dancing, my bony body
flailing like an uncaged bird. I repeated what my brother
and Ernie said: *Good idea*. And then I said *good idea*, and
this carried on until they both told me to shut up.

I had to beg them to let me play. When it was just my
brother and me, it took much less convincing. Typically,
my brother and I would be found in our bedroom fighting
for the video game console. If I was lucky, he'd give me the
extra Nintendo controller, and I'd slam the buttons down,
thinking we were playing together—that Mario was moving
just how I wanted him to move, though it was a one-player
game. If my brother was in no mood for sharing, I'd complain to Mom. This was a dangerous tactic. Sure, he'd be
forced to let me join, but when Mom was not around, he
would retaliate for getting him in trouble. My brother
wouldn't punch me hard enough that I bruised but hard
enough that I'd think twice before telling on him again.

.........

As charming as Aunt Sammy was, there was something odd
about her, something that unsettled me. Her face was the
soft kind of brown that looked fresh, almost lightly melted.

But there was almost a rigidity about her, as if she moved stiffly and mechanically. Mom told me not to stare. She said Aunt Sammy had an accident when she was younger, one that left her scarred. She had a metal plate in the front of her head. And though it was barely visible, I thought I could see where it would be. I studied the bulge on her forehead and was fascinated by its strangeness. I wondered if it was an antenna, if she could pick up radio broadcasts or a playing of *War of the Worlds*. Maybe she had telekinesis and could move things with her mind.

.........

With Aunt Sammy absent, Ernie, my brother, and I planned a footrace. We created the obstacle course first. We each tugged a couch cushion off the sectional sofa. Mine felt like a hundred pounds. I wobbled while trying to lug it. We stacked them in a corner alongside the couch. With the cushions gone, each of us gripped a metal bar that would support the pull-out mattress. We yanked it, taking the three of us using all our body weight, and slowly, the bed freed. Ernie mimicked the Transformer sound.

The frame groaned as it was fully extended. A puff of dust billowed, and the new bed smelled old. It wasn't much, a flimsy mattress with a thin, stained sheet cover. There were three impressions from where the bed had folded onto itself, for however many years, an origami of sorts. I thought about the bunk bed I shared with my brother at home, about the games we played, like using rubber bands to bungee jump action figures and drop parachute paratroopers from the top bunk.

The air in the house was smoky, like fallout from a collection of Aunt Sammy's cigarettes that hadn't burned out yet. Mom never smoked. I never even saw her with a beer. She was proper, in her own glamorous way: dresses, capris, boat shoes, expensive handbags, the inflection of her voice, as if always on some business call. In comparison, Aunt Sammy smoked, drank from forty-ounce beer bottles, wore ripped jean shorts and tank tops, and talked in a Southern slang I sometimes couldn't understand: *Go crank up dat car; I fin' to go to da store*—all of that. Mom would say that I needed to pronounce the *ing* in every present participle. So it seemed that the only thing Mom and Aunt Sammy had in common anymore was blood.

.........

When my brother wouldn't play with me, which was more often than not, Mom sometimes would. She'd say *back in my day*, and then we'd go back in her day and play jacks, like how she and Aunt Sammy played. When we did, I never saw Mom move so quick, swiping the jacks in seconds before the marble fell. Mom would tell me how close she and Aunt Sammy were, how she called her Big Sister Sammy, and Mom would tell me those same stories, about how no one messed with her when Aunt Sammy was around. Even though Aunt Sammy stood only four foot eleven, she was a powerhouse and wasn't afraid of anybody. She'd fight girls in the neighborhood, anybody who messed with her little sister. From bus stop brawls, to corner street scraps, Aunt Sammy was her protector, clenching collars, bruising bodies, taking names and not taking no lip. Mom told me that my big brother would do the same, even if he was mean to me. Back then, I wished my brother was more like Aunt Sammy, for if anyone was going to ball a fist at me, it would have been my brother.

.........

Ernie and my brother didn't ask me to participate, but I listened for the directions anyway: *Start in the kitchen, run into the living room, jump on the ottoman, then over the gap, onto the pull-out, over to that side of the couch, swing around, back into the kitchen. Whoever gets to the kitchen first, wins,* Ernie explained. And my brother was five years older than me, and my cousin was two years older than him, so my body literally was half the size of them both. Still, I swore that wouldn't stop me. So, I lined up with them, our feet on the imaginary line. When Ernie sounded his hand-made mouth horn, the three of us shot off.

Each step I took was twice as slow, and the distance between us lengthened. They left Wile E. Coyote dust clouds while cutting corners around the wooden chairs in the kitchen and then past the table. I tried to keep up, sprinting on the tips of my toes. We ran through the hallway, into the living room, the sounds of our feet like stampedes. Back near the couch, they hurdled over the ottoman. I used my hands to prop me up. On the ottoman, they took one bounce each, ricocheted, and sprung onto the mattress, and then over to the other side of the couch. Trailing behind, I hopped quickly from the ottoman and leaped.

I didn't make it far. Somewhere between the couch and the mattress, gravity or fear or distance took hold of me.

And like Icarus, I descended, falling face first into the metal frame of the pull-out bed. Ernie and my brother were celebrating in the kitchen, and I was like a red paint can toppled and staining that bedsheet. If I was crying, I couldn't hear it. My head echoed the percussion of a thousand tambourines. At some point when they finally looked behind and that shadow that had annoyed them all day was gone, they cheered more.

Aunt Sammy phoned for Nana. When Nana arrived, I was sitting on the mattress of the pull-out bed with a bloody, damp dishrag over my face. She drove me to the hospital. A big gash stretched over my right eyebrow. When the doctor came into my room, he said it needed stitches. It took fifteen to close the wound. *He probably has a concussion*, the doctor said, but Nana seemed more worried about Mom finding out. Afterward, Nana took me back to her house. And though my face was swollen and hurt, and the stitches frayed out from my eyebrow, I thought *at least, maybe I might look like Aunt Sammy*. I thought that we could compare scars, and maybe I'd have special powers too.

.........

Some weeks later when Mom came to get us from Nana's, she immediately noticed my injury. Nana, after however many phone calls, never told Mom what had happened. I was feeling much better though, and the swelling had gone down. In the last couple days, no one was mean to me, and my brother let me hang out with him and Ernie. And Aunt Sammy joked about giving me a taste of what she drank to ease the pain. But when Mom found out, she was livid. She took on a voice I rarely heard. She argued, demanded, threatened that she'd never let us go back to stay with Nana in Alabama without her again. Nana was not supposed to leave us at Aunt Sammy's because of that very reason: Aunt Sammy didn't take care of herself, much less watch us. Mom said she'd never let me visit Aunt Sammy again, and I never did.

Not until I was older did Mom tell me how Aunt Sammy got her scar. Mom said that when Aunt Sammy was about thirty, on one of those drunken nights when the darkness turned in on itself, that instead of returning home after a couple extra hours or even a day from binge drinking, Aunt Sammy hadn't returned. That some days later, Aunt Sammy was found in a ditch, bleeding and unconscious. That someone had mugged her. That someone hit her with a pipe, split her face open, and left her for dead. And that after the incident, Aunt Sammy was never quite the same.

.........

Aunt Sammy and I have the same birthday. She used to call me every year, and though the conversation wasn't much, it was special for us both. It was our connection, and maybe that's why I loved her so much, and why she was always kind and sweet to me, her birthday-nephew. She doesn't call me anymore—she can't. Now, I don't think she even remembers that we have the same birthday. Aunt Sammy had a stroke from all that life had done to her body, and I don't think she recognizes me. When her health started to deteriorate at sixty years old, she moved in with Nana. But

Nana was old too and could barely take care of herself. So, Aunt Sammy was sent to a nursing home. Mom said Aunt Sammy would be happier there.

And every year on our birthday, that scar of mine has healed a little more. Today, it's barely noticeable, and I think about it almost as much as I think about Aunt Sammy.

# ALABAMA FIRE ANTS

.........

NANA lived in a blue Creole cottage-style home in Alabama. The stars fell heavy on Alabama, so they say, but I remember the sun, and its lidless glare, staring above me as if an all-day fixation, like the sun wanted me to burn. My skin was much lighter than the rest of my family, a sandy beige. By Mom's orders, I had to wear sunscreen—no one else, just me—like a blotchy cover-up. And rightfully, I became the joke, my lightness and their heckling, just two words: *White Boy.* I was the *white boy* in a family of Black boys and Black girls, of Black men and Black women, and years of being Black in this stoic world made my skin some kind of leprosy. *White Boy can't jump. White Boy can't play. White Boy go back inside*, where *White Boy stays* because *White Boy* can't take the heat, can't run the ball, catch the ball, shoot the ball—*White Boy can't play.*

There is always a winner and a loser, an account of the victory, and the untold story of the loss. Our back-yard game of catch was no different. There was our captain, Kassidy, and the lackeys, us. Kassidy was the most loudmouthed, loose-tongued, disingenuous person I had ever met. She was the two-faced type to tell me I was her favorite cousin, and then, I was the white boy who lynched our great-grandparents. And yet, she spoke this so well, so sweet, almost in iambics: *If you should die we all will be happy.* She could sing hurt like a nursery rhyme. And we'd all listen to her words under some sovereign service as the shadow of a small curly-haired girl, like an effigy, stood splitting the sun into bright weaving waves of golden yellows over our faces.

Her right-hand man was my brother, Troy. His could never say no to Kassidy or defend me or anyone or anything else unpopular. Though he was my brother, Troy and I had different fathers. My father was white. His father was Black. We looked nothing like brothers. We could have been strangers from the way indifference occupied his silence. Sometimes when we were all outside playing and he walked ahead of me, I imagined him holding my hand in a fist of colors—of little bones and knuckles and dark skin leathered around my hand, like the way brothers are supposed to brother.

The other players were Ernie and Derrick. Ernie was the oldest of us, but he lacked the confidence to be a leader. His eyes were crossed like dark wobbling stones. His voice moved to the speed of the slowed shunt of an old train, and when he talked, it sounded like Otis Redding if the record were scratched. And then there was Derrick, a year older than me and my rival, always my opposition like two gravities. Derrick and Davon, a sensational fight, by no choice, faced off merely because of the humor of it all, or the way our bodies blurred browns and tans as if violence were a paintbrush. But who could blame kids being kids. Nana left us to ourselves somewhere behind her ears, outside her mind, outside her reach.

Kassidy established the rules, two teams: Ernie and Derrick on one, and Troy, Kassidy, and me on the other. Kassidy said the game was simple, in her most euphonic voice *elect one person from each team to go in the middle and both teams will throw the football back and forth. The lucky man in the middle will win the game, if he catches the ball.* It sounded exciting, especially because I was included. Often enough, I sat on Nana's stoop, with my legs crabbed, my glasses sliding down the bridge of my nose, and me watching everyone else play. My cousins would laugh and joke like the world and my exclusion from it was something funny. But now, Kassidy turned and affectionately pinched my cheeks and told me I was the man in the middle.

The brininess of their bodies like dark clothes drying on clotheslines; grass was wild and singed; the ground was corrugated; their knees were black; their muscular legs hardened and moved like uprooted tree trunks; their smiles grew large with room to still keep growing, and I watched the football soar in spirals above my head. My feet wobbled as I tried to find a steady position to jump for the ball. *White Boy in the middle.* With each pass, their banter cut like a scalpel removing the suture that kept me together, my family—family, which is supposed to be the stitch between the self and the world—but they furthered my separation. And yet still, I jumped and jumped.

Between both teams was a monstrous mound of earth, the telltale sign of a fire ant nest. Nana always warned us about them. She'd say that one fire ant's sting would burn for hours, and that fire ants don't sting just once, they sting until they decide to stop. The football continued soaring like their banter: *White Boy can't jump, White Boy can't jump, White Boy can't jump,* from Kassidy to Ernie to Derrick to Troy like some chain gang chant. I don't remember if I was crying or if it was sweat stinging my eyes, but I was leaping for that ball. And after what felt like an eternity or maybe just fifty tosses, I caught it. The leathery oval and the white laces rested comfortably in my hand. I celebrated and stomped my feet and smashed the mounded earth.

I thought the first squads of ants were just freckles sprouting about my skin, maybe the freckles were new or maybe they had just been there all along. I swiped at my leg. The pain didn't start, but there was movement. And in that moment when all the ants began to scatter like little clumps of dirt, my leg was like those in my family: it was dark, and it moved like soil. It was earth; my skin was this hot changing flesh like some kind of birth or death, and before the firing of all my nerves and the pain of hundreds of thousands of ants biting my leg with each ant's mandible anchoring into my skin and inserting a sting once and again, the pain, for that instant, in that moment, was worth it.

I remember standing, and my right leg from my foot to up my shorts was completely covered in ants. I was screaming from my gut. Someone yelled for Nana. She and my uncle rushed outside. I think I fainted then. I remember waking up in the bathtub, my pants off, and my twig legs trembling violently. The ants were still biting. They had risen to the elastic leg opening of my underwear. I don't remember blood, just swelling, an embalmment of the body. My uncle's big hands squeezed around my ankles to hold me still, and Nana poured iodine over my legs. The ants, like a swampy molasses, receded down the drain.

I avoided fire ants for the rest of that summer and spent my final days in bed, alone, with my right leg swollen, hot, ballooned, and covered in chalky calamine lotion.

.........

The summers after that when I returned to Alabama, I stuck nine-volt batteries in as many fire ants' nests as I could find. I'd wait for the batteries to warp. After a day or two, the sun's heat, like under a magnifying glass, caused the batteries to leak acid, and eventually, the ants scurried out their nests carrying little chunks of blister-brown earth—holding on as survivors who were barely surviving. I came to realize that it wasn't the ants' fault when they attacked me; they were protecting their queen. And maybe that's the strange nature of things—somehow if given the chance, the oppressed will always become the oppressor. So, I can't entirely blame my family and their mistreatment of me. In those Alabama summers when, though from different parts of America, we lived together at Nana's house, the didactics of race and color and its clear and almost honest separation of people affected us all—this thick axiomatic understanding in the way the Confederate flags whipped their arms off front porches, and the way these flags seemed to scream behind the exhaling exhaust of pickup trucks that never stopped as we crossed the roads. And the way a white face looked when smudged behind security glass at the corner store. And the same way the clerk with the tongue touching the red palate of their mouth called us all nigger, like some greeting, while ringing up our bags of chips, and the normality of it all, like racism is weather, and when it rains, bring an umbrella and walk that way—away from the Blacks on the sidewalk eating their bags of chips. And for my family, severance and its salt, this erosion of self, I was the constant reminder that between the Black and white is where I planted, and I stayed. While segregated in the Deep South, at Nana's house, fist-filled eyes broke bones, and words mosquito-stuck to bruised skin, and I was in the middle desperately trying to grab and hold on to something to call my own.

# DON'T OPEN THE DOOR

.........

WE lived in a two-level home, where the front door was textured glass, and every day was like looking into a window of a dark church. When we'd peek through the top, always before entering, I'd put my foot on my brother's knee, balance, stand, and everything looked warped, the hallway slick and shadowed. My brother and I shared this fear of what waited in that darkness inside, as if there was a buzzard squawking and flapping its hollow bones and one flight away from pecking our eyes out. Through the front door and to the left, was a short hallway leading to our landlord's apartment. When the coast was clear and she was nowhere to be found, we'd open the door and run up those percussive stairs to our apartment with fear and fire on our feet.

The landlord became our mystery. We swore she was a voodoo witch from a faraway island. Her skin was inky black, and her eyes were pure pupil. The depth and weight in her voice sounded like it came from someone else, some devil that possessed her speech and even her walk, movements always unbalanced like her body was foreign even to her. She scared me more than I could articulate, like the way a room does when the lights are shut off and you can't find the switch and just know that something is watching you—and whatever it is, is dark and bottomless and is a touch away from pulling you under.

She'd stump upstairs and bang at the door, her heavy hand was always one pound away from turning the wood into splints, *too loud*, she'd say repeatedly, demanding us to quiet. This never happened when our parents or big sister were home. It was as if she knew when we were home alone. And when we tried to tell Mom, she said we were overreacting. She said *be quieter and she won't bother you; she's old and works nights*. But we were not overacting because the boy who cries wolf was not only about dishonesty but also about the vulturous nature of predators, those sixth-sensed who smell the vulnerabilities in our blood. And those days when our sister left us home alone, barely ten and almost five, we swore we'd be dragged down into the landlord's apartment and never seen again except on the back of milk cartons. It was like the three of us held a secret and nothing about it was good.

.........

When our cousin, Ernie, was visiting, he insisted we find out for sure if the landlord really was a voodoo witch. We waited for her to leave one day, watching from a bay window. It was early afternoon by the time she slunk outside the apartment building as if she had just seen the sun for the first time in weeks. Tiptoeing, we slipped down those stairs. We had no plan. Ernie said if the door was open, we'd go in; if it was locked, we'd leave. My brother put on his thick fearless face, but I remember the patterns of sweat on the back of his shirt, each one growing bigger and fiercer. When we reached the door, the only thing keeping us from the darkness she owned was a twist of the knob. Ernie wiggled it, and the door creaked.

*You're our lookout*, Ernie said and told me to stay by the front door just in case she came home. So I stood by the entryway of the landlord's apartment. Ernie and my brother walked in the front door. I pretended my sweaty hands were binoculars. From the doorway, the living room was visible. A thick musk stifled the air. The apartment was lit with ebbing candles. Ernie turned to the right and entered a room. My brother turned to the left and entered a room. I peered through my binoculars.

After a few minutes, I heard noises coming from what must have been the kitchen, dishes and pots clanging and cabinets closing. We were wrong to think no one was home. Ernie and my brother heard it too and each slowly opened the door of the room they were searching. Fear distorted all our faces, for we now knew what was under the bed, and inside the closet, and behind the door: it was the real proof of nightmares, the things films were based upon, the panic that enters and cements you to time and all you can do is wide eye. I pointed in the direction of where the kitchen would be. The racket increased and footsteps followed.

The shadow of a body cast through the flickering candlelight. Ernie didn't wait to find out who it was. He ran and pushed past me while I was still peering in from the

hallway. I wanted to follow him, to run quickly back to
safety, but what about my brother? Maybe if I just stood
there for another minute, Troy could make the same escape.
I turned back to the apartment, and that shadow walked
into the living room. My brother quietly pulled himself
back into the room where he was hiding and slowly closed
the door. It was a man. The man investigated, panning his
dark head. His thin frame moved, the bones first, pushing
through the skin. He looked to the left, the room where
my brother was hiding. And then he looked to the right,
the room Ernie had just run from. He opened the door to
the right and walked in. My stomach bobbed in my throat.
I stifled a scream. The man walked out of the room and
looked in my direction. I spun my back against the wall
and tried to hide in the corner of the open door. He walked
toward the open door, his heavy steps hammering as loud
as my chest. The wood floor moved with him. He closed in.
When I could hear him breathe and feel the heat on me, he
slammed the front door shut.

I don't know how long my brother was in there, but I
waited outside the landlord's door and he didn't return.
I should have left, gone to get an adult, but I didn't;
I wanted to save my brother, but I could barely move. I
didn't even know what voodoo actually was. I didn't imagine strung-up and headless chickens. I didn't see bowls of
blood. I didn't imagine talc powder covering my brother's
body. I just knew he was in danger. If I rang the door-
bell or knocked, the man might take me too. What was
my brother doing? Was he still in the room? Maybe under
the bed? Was he safe? With my ear to the door, I heard

footsteps charge in my direction. The door swung open and my brother grabbed me and pulled me in a sprint. We ran up those stairs to our apartment like whatever this world was, it was moments away from being over.

.........

Ernie didn't need to convince us she was a voodoo witch. We knew it, and she would get us as soon as we were alone in our apartment. But with Ernie still there, we were brave and plotted booby traps and escape plans, much like the plot of *Home Alone*. A few days later though, after Ernie left, my brother and I were as paranoid as ever and on our best behavior, tiptoeing and whispering, trying to avoid the landlord. A week after the break-in, our sister said she was going to walk a friend home and that she would be right back and reminded us, as she always did, to lock the door and not to answer for anyone. Soon after we locked that door and sat on the couch and were watching cartoons and waiting for our sister to come home, we heard someone walking up the stairs to our apartment.

Each footstep planted for a moment before stepping again. These feet were patient and purposeful. My brother and I didn't budge but listened as if trying to measure the distance by the sound of the feet. The movement stopped for a while, and then a quick shuffle up the rest of the stairs. There was banging on the door followed by yelling. *I know ya' in there. Open da' door.* And we collapsed, hiding into our ribs, wrapping arms around each other for protection. My brother pressed his finger against my lips. I felt his heart on my back. More banging and yelling, *open da' door,* and we said nothing. It quieted, until who we knew was the landlord said *I have my own key.*

Of course, she had a key; she was the landlord. She knew we were in her apartment, and she knew what we discovered and couldn't let us live for it. My brother peeled my arms off of him. He shuffled to the door on the balls of his feet. He gripped the doorknob as hard as he could, his muscles tense and trembling. The doorknob attempted to twist from the other side. My brother countered. The knob turned, and he'd clench. This continued intensely until it stopped. My brother glanced back at me with a look of reassurance, as if to say *we're safe now.* And then, whatever relief we thought we had turned to more horror: a pair of scissors, blade first, jabbed under the door. They almost cut my brother's bare feet. His whole body panicked, flinching and dodging.

My brother let go of the doorknob, ran past the couch, and into our bedroom. I tripped off the couch and followed him. In our room, we scrambled for a place to hide. We stuffed ourselves under our sister's twin bed. From underneath, we could see the floor of the living room. The lock unlocked. The door opened, just a shadow first, pressing the rectangular darkness against a lamp light in the apartment. My brother drew me in closer, feeling the shakiness of my belly and the anxiety beating from his heart. The landlord walked in like a hot animal, breathing full and heavy, looking for prey.

We saw her legs hustle from corner to corner. We heard her quick shuffling, a pause, and then shuffling again. She was tracking us. I was convinced that fear could kill, that she would kill us. She walked toward our bedroom, about six feet from where we were hiding. Her arthritic-looking hands hung long and low like the blades from Freddy Krueger's glove. Her respirations excited. As if she knew she was close. As if she could taste our prepubescent sweat. One foot, another foot, and then she was in front of the bed. I could smell that musty scent from her apartment, like moist body, an uncooked and over-spiced piece of meat. She waited above us.

When the door of our apartment opened, we heard our sister scream *what are you doing? Get out!* The landlord pivoted and hustled into the living room. Our sister raced into the apartment. She was all brawn, her body was strong, and she was not one to argue with. Our sister could beat us both, even if tag-teamed, in a wrestling match. And the landlord, from what we remembered, was much smaller than her. So, in that living room, the two of them sized each other up, the way beasts do.

*I'm goin' to get all of ya*, my brother and I thought we heard the landlord say. She walked out of the apartment and our sister slammed the door behind her.

When our mom and dad came home, we told them the whole story, including breaking into the landlord's apartment. And our mom was livid, of course, but not entirely angry with us like we thought she would be. Rather, she was worried and anxious, and she considered calling the police. *But to apologize is ridiculous*, she said. *It is our apartment.* Though after she calmed some, we heard our mom and our dad say something about it being legal to enter if the landlord announced her entrance, and how we thought she never did. *But she tried to kill us, Mom. The scissors, Mom.* We tried to explain. Maybe our parents thought it was just an exaggeration.

.........

Some days later when our child-driven hysteria calmed and our parents had enough wild speculation, our dad saw something outside while we were eating at the dinner table. He stared through the blinds. He tilted them with his fingers, peeked, squinted, and saw something in that half-lit cast of yellow light that washed over the close to three-hundred-foot backyard. He called us over. Shoulder to shoulder, we looked out. Like apparitions in the oxidized floodlight, between the ground and weeds and shrubs, there were mounds of piled dirt, and near them, holes had been dug. And like focusing a camera, we squinted our eyes to see five empty plots, lined and ready. There was even a little grave dug for me.

# THE SETTLERS INN

.........

THE streets were almost empty, a few cars passed, each one driving leisurely. We lapped in circles: *Left here. No, right, right there. Stop. Is that it?* Our mom directed while peering from a large road map. Almost three hours from North Jersey to South Jersey, down the Turnpike, counted however many Volkswagen Beetles, sang about the wheels on the bus, and rock and paper and scissors and shoot—and the five of us, crammed, antsy, awaiting what might be our new home. But we were starving and couldn't focus. The traffic we hit on the Friday afternoon drive led us into the night. It was after dinnertime, and now we were looking for somewhere to eat.

Infrequent streetlights lit the street signs. My brother tried pronouncing the names, *Apache*, *Mohawk*, *Lakota*, *Lenape*. We were rubbernecking and finger-pointing tourists, amazed at what we saw, amazed at the differences from North Jersey to South Jersey, or urban versus rural-suburban. A sign my brother had never seen: *What is a "Deer Xing"?* Instead of apartment buildings, bus stops,

fast food restaurants, and bustling traffic, in front of us
were trees, real giant trees that crowded the roadsides, each
one in the hundreds and shoving the others for space—trees
that reached far into the sky and touched the dark clouds
that overhung in the soft turning twilight. We stopped at
an intersection, and little glimmers of moon skirted on
the surface of a body of water in the distance. The moon
and the water were silky, silvery, and silent. A sign read
"Welcome to Medford Lakes."

Our dad's brother lived in Tabernacle, a neighboring
town, and he told my parents *good schools, safe, secluded,
nice sized property.* This was not long after the wedding.
Prior to the potential move, Mom and Dad rented an apartment. But like any newlyweds, they wanted something for
themselves, a part of the American Dream: the piece of
land, the picket fence, the two-car garage. Mom, the nurse,
and Dad, the truck driver, did everything right, followed
the traditional trajectory: small wedding, cheap honey-
moon, saved money. Dad's brother said they could buy a
bigger house in South Jersey for the same amount they'd
pay for a smaller one in North Jersey.

Mom prefaced the move by telling us the house would
have enough space for a swing set, a basketball hoop, and
maybe we'd each have our own room. Regardless of how
big the house would actually be, we were convinced it'd be
a mansion. We chatted days before about all of the things
we would do: the hallways would be wide enough to pedal
a bike, the yard would be large enough to play hide-and-
seek and never be found, the forts we would build in the
basement and where we'd maybe camp out for days.

.........

We drove more, screeching around cul-de-sacs, K-turns on one-ways, hazard lights at stop signs. No familiarity, just a sedan as a caravan, a family of frontiers people pioneering through the New Jersey Pine Barrens.

We finally stopped at a place called The Settlers Inn, a giant log building that paralleled a lake and sat in the middle of two intersections. The measureless nature and its unending stretch wasn't fully comprehensible until we hopped out the car; we stood like we just struck land. The five of us looked up and around and backwards and sideways, and we felt small. It was impossible not to feel small, as if the trees and the bushes and the branches, and even the gray, sober sky was coming down on us. We were ants in a forest.

The size of the wooden complex was extraordinary, covering at least ten thousand square feet. Protruding from the roof, a chimney composed of countless stones. Windows on every facade of the building peered out into the partially developed wilderness. And hand over hand, eager and excited, we helped Dad pull the handle of the oversized door. It creaked loudly and expectedly, as if every door in this log building would perform the same.

Walking in and huddled together, the smell of wood awakened us. The oil from the lumber, like a porous fog, held invisibly to the air and to our noses. Two staircases conjoined to meet in a landing at the entrance near where we stood. The entire interior was wood or a replica of wood, from the walls that were the split bodies of some

giant trees to the light fixtures that were rustic and pasto-
ral, and even the pine-colored carpet that covered almost
all of the flooring. Everything from tablecloths to the paintings and decor personified a way of life so different than
ours.

Medford Lakes, Dad learned from a pamphlet, started
as a vacation town, and The Settlers Inn was both a res-
taurant and a lodge for travelers. Dinner tables scattered all
about the downstairs, and above that, an upper deck with a
long branching banister followed the walkways to the guest
bedrooms. We were seated near a fireplace, which was the
largest, if not the only, fireplace my sister, brother, and I
had ever seen. Constructed entirely of stone, the fireplace
was stationed as the centerpiece of the dining area. The
fire itself was massive, growing wild, primordial, and hellish. The flames fiercely licking the glass doors, as if trying
to escape. And in various parts of the hall, mounted deer
heads glared at customers, dark glassy eyes stared in bewil-
derment. And when we scanned the menu, Dad, in some
good humor, pointed to one deer on the wall and said *that's
for dinner.*

# TO BE A MAN

.........

A real man will sacrifice. He bleeds, and he sweats, and he dies. From sunup to sundown, he works till his skin is raw, till his eyes are glassed, till his heart is rock. At the end of the day, his back hurts, his bones are rebar, and he aches, as if something inside him is always broken. And yet, he has a tool for what seems to be any and every problem: his brain, an instruction manual, fixing things that rattle, things that smoke, bolts that are stripped that he somehow locks, he somehow always knows what to do, and maybe only God knows more, only God knows what he is made of, the workings of his body, the gears, the grooves, the way his arms are pulleys, the way his legs are iron, how his fists are hammers. Believe me, I've seen him work: coughing sawdust, wiping grease, picking splints from under his fingernails. I've seen him come home after a ten-hour shift of driving an eighteen-wheeler along the interstate, after hours of popping the clutch pedal, as if the truck and his bones became one, one machine, one body, like an extension of him, his job and his soul, the gasoline and his blood, fueling the same thing. And just to come home to work again, a man on empty, repairing the leak under the radiator, under the sink, behind the toilet, the cracked exhaust pipe, the scratched paint, whatever it was, never complaining. Because he's a verb, an action, a doer, a giver, irrefutably. Take his shirt, his pants, his boots, his time— take his life: he'd give it all and then again. It is his duty, he said so when he married my mother. He said so in a promise, a covenant, the man who would then love her three children as his own. As if he were their father, an eleven-, six-, and one-year-old, all with different fathers. But that didn't matter; it never mattered that they weren't his real children. Because he swore to them when we swore to her, when he swore to God on the altar. And I hope to be a real man like him.

# PATRICIDE AND BOOT SHINES

.........

ONE day I will ask my mother about my father, and she will lie. She will tell me Daddy is in the other room shining his boots, and I will nod my little head and scramble two twine legs into the other room and ask Dad why he shines his boots. I will say *Dad, what for?* He will smile and press his large hand to mat my whirling curls. He will offer me the faded rag, and I will help him shine his boots. I will shine those boots like I've shined boots all my life. But one day my mother will kill my daddy. She will tell me *he is not your father.* I will not understand, and I will cry. He won't be in the room while my face dampens the waist of her dress because I know no one will shine Daddy's boots. My mother will show me a picture. I will not see myself. I will say *no*, until the picture dies. She will knot me in her arms. I will mourn like I know what death means. She will take me to some park to meet my father. My arms will cross over my seatbelt for two hours, and my eyes will puff and swell. I will say *not my daddy*, and I will want to kill him. But my father will wait underneath a tree. I will unfasten my Velcro-strap shoes. My lips will salt, my nose will bubble, and I will sprawl my body like a wet bird. I will scream *not Daddy*, and the man will smile.

# WITH MY DAD

.........

TUCKING my bedsheets in tight, you start at the bottom, where my feet are sticking out. You tell me how big I'm getting. Your hands are irons pressing the seams flat while I'm cocooned and worming around. You fluff my pillow, and turn it on its back, where it's the coldest. Then you make a cape out of the blanket, and fly, humming Superman's theme song. I laugh like I'm being tickled. And after five or ten whooshes, you look at your watch, put your cape down, and tell me it's time for bed. *But Dad, please*, I beg, tossing and turning, hoping to get my way. And then you give me one more triumph, *dun-da-dah*, and turn back into my superhero.

.........

You shake the Polaroid photo. You're watching my two-finger peace sign appear from the cloudy film. I'm a little boy out of the past. Shake it more. You can see the stone driveway, and my light-up sneakers flash red around the bottom rims. We are here. This new home. We're waiting for the school bus on the first day of school. And which of you scribbled my name on my nametag? This is your ownership. I am your son. Standing barely three feet, and my backpack is just as large. And maybe my smile makes the photo appear quicker, or you shake it harder, in some anticipation of seeing me again.

.........

You and Mom are dressed up for Back-to-School Night. All the parents are tunneling through the front entrance of the building. They're chattering and holding notebooks. I begged you to let me come. I'm proud to show you off. Other parents brought their children too: *Look, Mom and Dad. Look, I told you.* I walk right in the middle of you both, holding hands like two ends of a jump rope. When we count to three, you lift me in the air, and you and Mom hold on to each side of my arms. I swing for a second. I'm starting school again. You prepared a list of questions, Mom too. *What will he be reading? How much arithmetic? Who are his teachers?* But I tell you I'll be okay, how I'm ready, and a big boy now, and I pull up the sleeve of my polo shirt and give one mighty bicep-flex. *Don't you worry*, I tell you. That little muscle trembles there for a while.

.........

It's Career Day. There's a doctor, a policeman, a businesswoman, a dentist, and each have a prop: stethoscope, handcuffs, laptop, false teeth. We are waiting our turn. My teacher gave you the same chair I have, and you look odd, sitting like a child. I'm anticipating our introduction, and as proud as ever to hang on to the word *my* like how *its* is possessive. And when the teacher calls us, wearing our matching ties, the ones with the chattering teeth, I run to the front of the classroom. I'd promised to stand straight and tall, with my head right by your belt loop that I always tug. And in front of the class, you name the different teeth on a dental skull, pointing with a pencil. Some kids are missing theirs and stick their tongues out and wiggle them through little gaps, excitingly. And they're wishing they had a dad as cool as mine.

.........

I chose the white Power Ranger. I spent the last week practicing my karate moves. Holding my fists, hands, and feet, you demonstrated the low-block, the high-block, the punch, and the roundhouse kick. I've even mastered the *swoosh* sounds my strikes will make, cutting the air with precision. And in between each strike, I will yell *kiai* from my belly. And while at school, I'm wearing a white ninja helmet with dark eye coverings, a white suit with a black-and-gold chest shield, and I'm carrying a plastic sword with a tiger engraved on it. At noon, all of us dressed in our Halloween costumes will parade around the perimeter of the school in front of our families, and the loudspeaker will play "Monster Mash." We'll march in lines, and when we do, I know you will be there in the best spot with your video camera ready and holstered on your shoulder. And when you see me, you'll say my name the loudest and shout *hooray*. You'll be waving. And I'll face the camera and do my best one-two-three-four combo: low-block, high-block, punch, and roundhouse kick.

.........

All of my friends from school are here. We rented a party room at the Fun Zone. The energy is high, kids rocking in miniature chairs, parents talking loudly over the kids, and our party-leader shouting between her horn-shaped hands. We're hyper from drinking what seems like an endless supply of Hawaiian Punch. We start chants, impatient but well organized: *Laser tag, laser tag, laser tag.* We're unruly, the party table becoming a bongo set. And in the room, wrapped presents and gift bags are pillars stacked in the corners and cards with my name on them. I'll have new toys and money to buy new toys for the entire year. It feels like the best day of my life. And before letting us out like an eager pack of puppies, our party-leader demands a group photo. Simultaneously, we all sigh and groan until our parents jam everyone together like a box of crayons. We smile big and wild, showing our teeth, not caring if any are missing. You're kneeling next to me and so is Mom, and you squeeze my shoulder, lovingly pressing me to your chest.

.........

And while none of this is true, these are some things I wish we did.

# FIGHTING FOR THE TREE

.........

BUT there were too many trees out back, some so high they were dangerous. If any one of those passing storms came, the storms that had torn roofs and stripped shingles, our sky-high oaks would most definitely rip out their roots and crash into our home. It was a serious fear for the local homeowners, since we all lived in the same Pine Barrens, the place where trees were as high in the sky as birds and birds were more frequent than deer and everyone owned almost an acre. Out back there was one tree that had to go, Dad said so, and he was going to do it himself. Dad said he didn't need to pay someone to cut down a tree. He had a chainsaw, an axe, a pruner. *The same tools the professionals use.* Dad and Mom argued over it because what man wants to be told he's not man enough to cut down a tree? Dad could fix cars as easily as he could split wood. *This would be simple*, he told her.

I wanted to help, and sometimes he'd let me. I could be useful, run for a different Philips-head screwdriver or

an adjustable wrench. Whatever the task, I'd do it. Often
though, I grabbed the wrong wrench or drill bit, and Dad
would send me again until he was annoyed enough to do
it himself. Not that Dad was cruel when frustrated by my
inability to follow directions, it was just easier to do it
himself, a skill he learned from his father and from his
grandfather, a line of do-it-yourself men. I could barely do
anything myself. I needed help opening a jar of jelly. Maybe
I was weak or had no resilience—blame my nerves, attention span, or because I was not like Dad.

.........

I sat on the deck, watching Dad prepare to cut down the
tree. He measured the width of it, stepping back with the
measuring tape, adjusting. With a can of spray paint, he
marked it, about waist-high, with an orange X. *What's that
for, Dad*, I called from the deck. *So I know exactly where
to cut. If I cut too low or too high, the tree might fall in the
opposite direction, right over there, on you.* I squirmed at
the thought. He said *gotta get it just right.* Mom told me
I had to watch and said *sit your butt down.* I wanted to
help, but there was nothing I could do from over here. *Dad,
Dad, can I get you anything?* I stood, my voice reaching
out between my two hands, and then some birds wrestled
and flew from out of the treetops. He wiped his brow, sweat
glazing his face. *A big cup of water with ice.* I nodded, ran
inside, searching for the largest cup I could find.

.........

I often thought Dad was always disappointed in me. I couldn't do anything right. When he asked me to help carry in groceries, handing me a gallon of milk: *Davon, are you sure you got this?* About halfway before getting to the kitchen with the container cradled in both arms like holding a bomb, I stumbled and dropped it in the garage, milk everywhere. The same thing happened when I carried in a watermelon. It was too heavy and plop, the watermelon fell and exploded across the floor. One would think Dad would learn and not ask for help. But if he didn't, I complained to Mom, and she'd make him. He could never say no. Even if he wanted to, Mom insisted I help. She'd make him take me to the store with him, rake the lawn, wash the cars—spend father-and-son time.

Mom had ultimate jurisdiction. She was the disciplinarian, the judge and jury. If I did something wrong, talked back, or cursed, Dad could only make empty threats. *Davon, go to your room. You're grounded.* Instead, I'd go find Mom and twist around the reason why I was in trouble in the first place. He'd be even more upset and annoyed when Mom sent me back down again to help him with whatever he was doing. That was the way of our relationship, a triangle of pointed fingers: *Davon stop; Dad stop; both of you stop.* I was infuriatingly sensitive, whining or crying anytime he upset me. Like when he teased me, coining the name Mr. Spiller for every time I spilled something. And when I did, which was often, he'd sing *Mr. Spiller, Mr. Spiller* and I'd throw a fit, stumping my feet, shouting, my eyes swelling with tears.

.........

I completed my mission, delivering Dad the biggest cup of ice water ever. Behind me, a trail of ice cubes. I ran it out to him, holding it in two hands, a giant 7-Eleven Big Gulp cup. He drank it quickly, wiping his mouth on his knuckles, the tough skin on the thick bristles of his mustache making a scratchy sound. He dropped the cup near the tree, where he had lined his tools by order of first use: pruner, axe, chainsaw, and bungee cord. Standing beside him, I wondered why he picked that tree, how he knew that one had to go. It was as if Dad knew things other people didn't know, a second intuition for how things worked, how the world worked. I imagined Dad could be stranded in the woods with only a knife and could survive for weeks, finding food and building shelter. It was how he thought, practically and pragmatically, a problem solver. I wanted to be like that; although, I was terrible at pragmatic thinking, like those word-problems in school about width and length. Give Dad a pencil, paper, and a ruler, and he could design a house, cubit by cubit. Give me a pencil, paper, and a ruler, and I could draw our family and write our story.

.........

I thought maybe I wasn't the son Dad wanted. If he could have chosen *this kid* or *that kid*, he'd pick the other, the son he'd enjoy. They could build things, wear matching tool belts, read how-to books, and cut down trees. I wanted to be that kid. I wanted to like cars and love the smell of gasoline. I wanted to like Home Depot, to search through those aisles as if finding ourselves, finding our eyes in the shades of paint, our skin in the tones of wood, and our hearts in the steel frames of rolling tool chests. I wanted to be like Dad even though I wasn't. I wanted to look like Dad even though I didn't. I wanted to think like Dad even though I couldn't. I wanted the same last name as Dad even though I wouldn't. And no matter how much I loved him, how much Mom encouraged our relationship— or I called him Dad and he called me Son, we always would have this difference between us.

.........

I wore my good clothes, collared shirt and khaki shorts. We were going to lunch and a movie, my father and me. I could say I was excited, but I wasn't sure how I felt, if I wanted to go with him or if I wanted to stay with Dad. It was incredibly complicated. Dad had been my father for seven years. My father was only around for the last three years, when our visitations began. How could I ever choose, like choosing a new friend over an old friend. The new friend, the new dad, bought me things: toys, waffles with ice cream, extra-large popcorns, giant movie-theater soda cups, the ones I could drink through the entire movie. And this *friend* never yelled or teased me, and maybe we looked alike, and we had the same last name, and Mom said he liked painting and drawing like me. But Dad was my everyday father. He raised me. He taught me how to ride my bike and tie my shoelaces. He cooked dinner and helped me with my math homework. We passed the soccer ball, and he chaperoned field trips. So what if he yelled at

me? He was still my dad. Those two men defined father-
hood very differently: one was a father and one fathered,
an *is* and a *does*.

My father never visited our house. Instead, Mom and I
drove to Hackensack, a two-hour drive, to visit him once a
month. On the way, I'd ask Mom why he never came to us.
She'd say because my father was much older than her, and
the long drive was too much, and one time he fell asleep
behind the wheel. I thought it was because of Dad, though,
that maybe the two didn't like each other. Maybe they both
loved Mom too much and couldn't be in the same room.
I wondered if there was bad blood. Would they fight over
me? But today, for the first time, he was on his way to see
me, and part of me was eager to show him around, show
him my room, my bike, my action figures, point out my
school and where I waited for the bus, the places I hung out
with my friends, the swing set and the basketball hoop. I
wanted to show him my world.

. . . . . . . . .

Dad looked into the branches. The pruner, like a massive third arm, reached high into the thicket of boughs.
He began sawing off stems and tree limbs. His concentration was deep, focused, methodical. His eyes were rulers,
mentally measuring *how much there, how much here*. If
it wasn't for his shirt's whiteness, he'd appear to be one
with the thick trunk, the bark and his skin almost the same
color. Heat flooded through the treetops. Sunlight radi-
ated in rip currents. I had already filled his water cup three
times. And on the deck, I sat still, my hands on my knees,

admiring Dad and listening to the sawing of the serrated blade and the reverberations of insects rubbing their little legs and the birdcalls from many places far in the distance. It always sounded like this, wonderful and harmonious.

When my father arrived, I ignored the engine's humming. I ignored the way the car idled, as if it were waiting for me. I heard my father's feet crunch on fallen leaves as he followed the sounds of the blade and walked out to the back. I waited until he was in front of me. I ignored him at first. Mom, from behind, lightly placed her hand on my back. *You ready, honey?* I was not ready. I wanted to help Dad. I stayed put, gritted my teeth, planted my heels, cemented in defiance. Mom's round of her thumb stopped its gentle circling, and she tapped my head. *Your father drove a long way to see you.* Her touch took on her tone. I didn't want to upset my father. *But what if Dad needs help*, I thought. My eyes avoided my father and darted to the tree, to Dad, and then to the ground. My chest rose and fell heavily. Mom kneeled to my level and quietly said *Dad won't be upset. You can help him when you come home.* My father stood patiently, observing gently, the way a photographer would.

After a few minutes, turning to Dad, my father said *hey, you need a hand?* Dad was standing in a pile of leaves and branches. The pruner gripped in his hand like a giant scepter. Dad craned his head to get a better look, his hand over eyes, blocking the sun, and said *Harry, you wanna help?* Dad gave the enormous tree a long stare, considering my father's request. *Sure, Harry. If you don't mind.* And then my father untucked his shirt from his pants and walked toward Dad. On his way over, he turned to me: *Do you mind, Davon?* I looked at Mom, wide-eyed, and shook my head. My smile grew uncontrollably.

The handshake seemed longer than normal, the two just standing there with hands clasped like stones. Maybe Dad was squeezing my father's hand harder, or maybe my father was squeezing Dad's hand firmer, maybe it was a standstill of strength. This was not the first time they met, but it was the first time my father was at our house. Dad did appear proud to show him around the yard, pointing in directions, talking farther away than I could hear. It was almost an acre of land, but we lived on only about a quarter of it, the rest was deeper in the backyard, uncharted, unruly, unmanageable, and full of ticks. Mom never let me back there. But Dad and my father ventured farther into the brush and shrubbery, below the pines and oaks, and into our private woods of the Pine Barrens.

*The movie can wait*, Mom said with approval. I was still on the deck, now quickly losing sight of my two dads as they traveled through the trees. Mom scooted my little butt over and sat next to me. I wondered how she felt, what she was thinking watching these two men. At the time, I didn't consider if she could love them both—not how I defined love, which was emotional, intimate, with kisses and hugs. But then again, I don't think you ever stop loving someone, or stop having love for them—especially the father of your child. Though it was guaranteed she loved Dad, this I knew. I was there when they promised, at their wedding, five years earlier. I even hand-delivered the rings on a heart-shaped cushion when they said *I do*. Dad and Mom had been together for as long as I could remember, and before I could remember, since I was a year old. Dad had always been my father, long before Harry ever called me his son.

.........

When they returned, Mom and I were shouldered next to each other. Dad called out *it's time to cut this tree down.* He and my father stood under the tree. Dad kneeled and gripped the chainsaw. Excited, I jumped to my feet. *Mom, can I go over there?* My whole body, a magnet, pulling to their position. *No, honey. You have to stay here, just in case the tree falls.* Like a puppy on a leash, I tried to inch farther when the chainsaw's motor ran, *brum-brum-brum-brrrrrrrr.* Mom drew me toward her. Dad put on a pair of safety glasses and earplugs from his jeans' pocket. He sent a thumbs-up our way. He said something to my father, and then my father, with his arms crossed, sauntered two steps back.

With his feet shoulder-width apart, Dad wielded the chainsaw like a weapon. Where he'd earlier spray-painted the X , Dad drove the saw into the mouth of the tree. Splints and sawdust billowed like the tree was coughing out its insides. Dad thrusted it in further, an unrelenting roar. Mom covered my ears. I swatted at her hands. *This is so cool,* I told her. After a minute or so, Dad pulled out the chainsaw. The tree had the smile of a jack-o'-lantern. He investigated, panning his head. And then my father said something to him. Dad shrugged, silent for a moment, and nodded.

My father picked up the axe. Now Dad stepped back. My father checked the weight of the axe, tossing it a couple times in and out his hands as if to say *this axe will do*. He squared up with the bole, where the bark grinned sinisterly, and swung with all his might. The wood croaked and begged for mercy. He jolted from his hips, through his arms, and into the tree, tirelessly. It became rhythmic, the blade hitting the wood. I was excited, looking at my dads and back at Mom, who appeared more nervous and worried. My father stopped, and the last crack echoed. The tree began to sway. He treaded backward. Mom clenched my arms tightly. The wind that hadn't affected the tree earlier now pulled it with an invisible elasticity, whispering *I'll finish the job*.

Both men yelled different directions. It went one way and then the other, as if a table losing one leg. Dad and my father, quickly moving on either side of the trunk, tried to balance it, but their strength was in no way effective. *Rope, rope!* The bungee rope was coiled in with the pile of tools. I wrestled out of Mom's grip and ran over to the rope, about twenty feet from the tree. I looked up, and it was frightening, the tree, a giant looming over me. Dad and my father, each with one hand on the tree and other open, in my direction, both yelled *throw me the rope!*

.........

I gave Dad the bungee, and it took him less than thirty seconds to wrap it around the tree. Mom yelled for me to return, and I ran back more fearful of her than of the tree. He repositioned himself with the bungee in hand, adjacent to the opening in the trunk. My father joined him, and as if one body, only inches apart, both men gripped the rope toward the same direction, tugging it with fear and desperation, away from the house. And together, Dad and my father fought that tree.

# WEEKEND WEATHER

.........

UNDER the weight of the toppling sky and the volume of sharp rains and the hard yells of my parents shaking the grout between the bricks of our home—on many of those nights, I was dust clung to those shaking corners, while Mom and Dad pushed and pulled their bodies into each other. And when they spoke, it was of divorce, and it was like the weather on weekends: *Maybe it'll rain, maybe I'll leave, maybe I don't love you.* I watched their shadows bounce beneath the crack from their bedroom door. Dad reminded her that she was never home, that *you are my wife, and you should be home, and you must love me for always and forever.* Those bedroom walls were thin, and if asbestos could have grown anywhere, it grew there. And when he yelled, Mom never hid. She squared up and told him *mind your damn business. I'm a grown-ass woman. You can tell me when to be home and where to go when you make enough damn money for me to not have to work.* My knees were hot and glued to my chest. I was a ball of bones cradling back and forth somewhere between the door and the doorframe, while my parents were unstable, like air that is unstable, like air that is hot, air that is cold, like air that is always gusting and pulling into each other, like air that is building and brewing and becoming something else—this air, and how it would rise, like how my parents' voices rose, how their bodies seemed to form into each other, how then, the violence of emotions was loud and thunderous, how this thing possessed them, how they moved just like those clouds that hung low and above our house, how then, my parents and their judgment, too, got clouded. Dad bargained for the phone by slamming his fist, and Mom said she would give him the phone after she called the police. Her *I wish you would* thunder-talk only tightened his jaw and blared his bark, until her mouth became her whole body and his hands became his mouth, and then we all shook at once, like a family.

# O. J. AND THE WAX MUSEUM

.........

AFTER my mother reported the racist incident to the state board of education but before the school's principal and superintendent retired as a result of the news channel's investigation, our mother told Troy that he could have been anyone, but if he wanted to portray a Black man then maybe portray Michael Jordan. She said Michael Jordan was a role model and exemplified the project's requirements. He could have worn Michael Jordan's jersey, Chicago Bulls, ninety-five. Michael Jordan was everyone's hero, especially Black boys, and my brother was a Black boy. But Troy's teacher, who did not look like him, had told Troy to portray O. J. Simpson in the 1995 Eighth Grade Wax Museum.

.........

In the annual eighth grade wax museum project, students chose a person or persons from current events and created a scene with a set, props, wardrobe, and caption with a three-page summary. The sets, once finished, would be displayed in the school cafeteria for parents and families to observe and vote on as the students were frozen in their roles as wax statues. Students spent weeks working on the project every year.

There was a lot happening in America. There were space shuttles, computers, anthropologic discoveries, NAFTA, but there were also bombings, killings, and murders. These were eighth graders, though, thirteen- and fourteen-year-olds, not adults, not the *Nightly News* watchers but children who could barely stand long enough to be like wax.

Troy could have chosen to be Bill Gates. He always liked computers. We even had an IBM, and Windows 95 had just been released. Troy spent hours trying to take that computer apart and put it back together. Maybe Bill Gates was already taken? But even if Bill Gates wasn't taken, Gates was never suggested. Computers were a current event, but to be Gates, would Troy have had to paint his skin, part his hair, change the inflection of his voice? Would it have been too unbelievable?

It was all make-believe anyway. When we tell kids to make-believe, do we want them to imagine, explore the possibilities, or do we really mean *be exactly who you are, what you are*? Is that why we tell little Black boys that they must be little imitations of Black men—that Troy could be Bill Russell, but not Bill Gates? *Maybe you should pick someone else*, we say, *who looks like you*.

O. J. Simpson had once been a quality role model. Over the course of his career, he had won the Heisman Trophy and was the NFL's Most Valuable Player of the year. He rushed for over two thousand yards and broke countless other records. He starred in films and was on the cover of magazines. He was an obvious example of Black excellence for Black boys. But it was 1995, and O. J. was on trial for murder.

Troy could have said no to his teacher. He could have gone home and told our mother that he felt uncomfortable portraying O. J., and maybe he really knew who O. J. Simpson was and what he stood for. Maybe the backlash with the news cameras could have been easily avoided. Troy could have spoken up for himself, the thirteen-year-old boy. He could have put his foot down and demanded not to be stereotyped, to be allowed to make his own choice, to be who he wanted to be.

The assignment required students to work in groups of three or four. After agreeing to portray O. J., Troy was joined by three other students, each as unsure about what to present as my brother was. The trial was inescapable. The news outlets spent every minute covering the story. It was good American television. But what did these kids really know? What did anyone really know? Everything was speculative. Except the grisly crime itself: who was murdered, where they were murdered, how they were murdered, what was left behind. So, when Troy and his group met to discuss their showcase, they unanimously agreed to recreate the crime scene.

The Wax Museum was the chatter of the entire school. Eager sixth and seventh graders hypothesized who they would pick, what they would do when they were in the eighth grade. The eighth graders, as excited as they were, tried to keep their projects secret. The students planned their projects in class but could only work on the sets and costumes at home. Troy and his group planned very little until the final days leading up to the showcase, maybe because they were reluctant, or lazy, or because they didn't know how to recreate a murder scene. While the other groups reportedly spent hundreds of dollars of their parents' money at the local arts and crafts store, Troy's group had to be resourceful. They made a list of clothing and props they could utilize from each other's houses. The list read something like *suit, sheet, briefcase, shorts, sandals, tank top, gloves, something for the blood.*

.........

When the big day finally arrived, the first showing was held during school. Students and teachers studied each exhibit, judging them according to category: Most Creative, Most Realistic, Most Waxlike, Best Set Design, and Best Costumes. For the audience, there were rules: no touching the exhibits, no touching the students, no talking or making faces—rather, be quiet and walk in a line. The students from the different grade levels channeled in, snaking single file, their *awws* all sounding the same. As the teachers viewed the exhibits, they stared silently, judging and evaluating, marking things down on paper. The presenting students posed from all different positions behind stanchions, next to their projects, each one trying their best to be waxlike—gritted teeth, squinting eyes, muscles tensed, some standing, some sitting, some lying—each of them holding their breath, hoping to win.

There was a group dressed in puffy sweatpants and

sweatshirts with handwritten logos that said *NASA*. The rumor was they used five entire boxes of aluminum foil to make their costumes. Another group brought in a desktop computer and sat in desk-armchairs around it, pointing with pencils and pretending to script notes on memo pads. They wore glasses, pocket protectors, and hung a handmade poster-sized Microsoft logo. So, Bill Gates had already been taken. On a makeshift football field, four boys, two in San Francisco 49ers jerseys, the other two representing the San Diego Chargers, created a pileup for an iconic touchdown. Other groups were scattered along the perimeter of the cafeteria, all reenacting something important, something museum-like.

In the middle of the room was my brother's group. A Black boy in a brown suit stood carrying a suitcase and a pair of leather gloves while walking away from two other boys lying on the floor, their bodies concealed under a bloody bed sheet. A little farther back, another boy stood watching the scene from a distance. The caption read, *O. J. Simpson murders ex-wife Nicole Simpson and her boyfriend Ron Goldman, leaving behind one suspected witness—O. J.'s houseguest, Kato Kaelin.*

If anyone was appalled, it wasn't noted at the principal's office. Instead, my brother's group received praise for the depiction, for its graphic but faithful rendition of the crime scene. Teachers voted anonymously. Rumor was that his group had racked up plenty of votes to win Most Realistic. But winners wouldn't be announced until the next day, because after the Wax Museum was staged in school for students and teachers during the day, the students returned for a second showing that night for their families. At 6:30, the show would begin.

When Troy got home after the first show, he knew he finally had to tell our mother about his scene. He knew his mistake was not just in portraying O. J. Simpson but also in not telling our mother he was portraying O. J. Simpson. All he had said leading up to the event was something like *I'm playing a football player, Mom, and I need a brown suit.*

Troy waited until that night to tell her the truth. He waited, maybe because he was shy or scared, or because he knew she would otherwise not have allowed him. She would have said no from day one. She would have been furious that he hadn't stood up for himself. She would have been ashamed, called the school, embarrassed him. Then, he wouldn't have had a group to work with. He would have let his friends down, and they wouldn't want to be his friends anymore. Everyone at school would have known. So, when Troy finally told her that he was going to be O. J. Simpson, she responded just how he expected her to. She also contacted *Action News*, on our local news station.

.........

Troy begged her not to make him go back for the school's evening program. He said he'd just take the failing grade. *Mom, please*, he said, with puddling eyes. But her mind was made. She, my brother, and the local news channel would meet at the school, where she would confront his teacher and principal. She dragged him by the arm, and they got in the car and drove to the school, where the white news van was waiting. Families arrived, chatting eagerly, while my mother and Troy and the people from the news channel trotted into the school with fire on their feet. My mother muttered lots of things under her breath, about her son, and *how dare they*, and *they won't get away with this*, and when she finally got to the door of the school, she stopped, took one deep breath, as if to compose herself, and turned to face the camera.

.........

My brother earned a reputation after the Wax Museum. The kids at school said, whenever there was adolescent drama—a fight at the bus stop, an argument in the cafeteria, a scuffle in gym class—*Troy, is your mom gonna to call the news again?* He went along with the joke, a cool jest that rolled off him in the hallway chatter, in the locker room, at the lunch table. The consequence, it seemed, was only ridicule from his classmates, an embarrassment that lingered like that one kid who was still teased for peeing his pants in kindergarten. But instead of the typical adolescent and teenage embarrassment, my brother was compared to a murderer, and my brother's name and reputation at the school became synonymous with O. J. Simpson.

# STEVE URKEL, KICK THE BALL

.........

THEY thought I'd be the best kid on the team, made plans before the season started, me at striker or wing using my speed to split defenders, inside scissors to a step-over, rotating the ball from heel to toe like a dance, like the move was made for me. *Might not need much coaching, just a couple drills—practice doesn't always make perfect.* Especially when you look like me. If they'd looked like me maybe they could have played in college, they thought. But this was middle school, the tryouts for the club team, and my parents had just bought me Adidas cleats and pull-up shin guards. I was ready to compete.

I shouldered for space from the other boys, touched my toes to stretch my calves, doubled-wrapped the long laces of my cleats around the midsole, and waited in the bulwark of boys for the whistle to blow. When it did, it pierced us like a flock of foraging birds. We released in a stampede. The goalkeeper, a kid in a yellow mesh jersey, cleared the ball, and it rose higher than the sun rises, and it filled the washed-out morning blue of the September sky—the

sky that was still a little humid and heavy and wet—and I
waited for the ball to fall and find me.

Tryouts had begun.

We started with traps. The goalkeeper sent another
punt. We chased the ball as the coaches yelled out different body parts. Trap with your chest, *punt*, trap with your
thigh, *punt*, inside foot, then put it all together—head,
chest, thigh, inside foot, pass, a rhythm. It was a fight for
the ball, bony bodies bumping into each other followed by
high-pitched grunts, *it's mine*, and the swish of our shuffling soccer shorts. In the distance, the coaches, two mid-
dle-aged men, chatted behind clipboards, calling names
and checking their paper.

The number of boys on the field dwindled as the coaches
waited for each of us to have a chance to trap the punted
ball. The goalie sent balls like shooting canons. I was afraid
the ball would knock me over, so when he punted, I jumped
out of the way, hoping the ball would roll to me. The ball
seemed to eclipse the sun, and I jumped again with no other
kids for me to hide behind, and stretched my body and led
with my head. Like a stone, that ball nearly toppled me
over and sent my glasses tumbling to the field.

The coaches announced our second drill. They placed
orange discs at the midfield where one coach stood with the
other coach stationed at the goal box. With his whistle in
his mouth, the midfield coach called four kids to the goal
box for the first wave of sprints. He listed off the names
and called out *Loeb*. I was shocked to be back on the field
immediately after blundering my last attempt. We met at
the goal box, standing four feet apart, and were to sprint

to the discs, run back to the starting line, and then to the opposing goal box. The same coach, still teething his whistle, pointing to his brows with a pencil, asked *Loeb, you need to keep your glasses on, right?* My voice cracked: *Yes, coach.*

We positioned—staggering our feet, tightening our laces—and some kid in the bunch on the sideline that was waiting for the next wave said *run four-eyes,* and a few of those kids shaped circles out of their fingers and stamped them to their faces. They peered at me, their mouths opened, their voices snickered in laughter. I pretended to ignore them, and I readjusted the nosepiece on my glasses.

The grass was still wet, and with each stride, grass was spitting in the air. By the time I arrived at the discs, of course, I placed last. The other boys were barely out of breath while I was keeled over, my glasses sliding off my face again. The coaches studied the four of us, mumbled their comments behind their clipboards, and commanded: *Sideline, boys.* They called out the next group. I jogged to the sideline, knowing some ridicule was forthcoming. When I approached, trying not to make eye contact, the boys put back on their finger-glasses.

After sprints, we arranged in groups of three to practice passing combinations: inside foot, outside foot, and any other passes we could think of. We met in the middle and stepped five strides backwards to form a circle. We rotated the ball, tapping with the insides and outsides of our feet. This finally felt easy, and I perked up, smiling between passes. I hit my partner's marker, the inside of his foot, and he said *good pass, dude.* It was a good pass, and I knew it and thought I might make the team. This was a big deal. In our small South Jersey suburban town, everyone played soccer, and not making the team was like being picked last in gym class or sitting alone in the lunchroom. This was my chance to be *in*, to be a part of something.

In the same groups, our coaches announced another drill before we could take a break. To mimic real action, we had to juggle and pass the ball as a group without letting it hit the ground for forty-five seconds, using our heads, chests, knees, and feet. Once each juggling group finished, we'd break on the sideline. We were to practice the drill for a couple minutes, and then when ready, call one of the coaches over to time and evaluate us.

There was a stud in my group, one of those kids who jumped for the ball and always found it—like the ball found him, something magnetic. He started the juggle by himself, popping the ball on his foot, holding it between midsole and ankle, and then up to his knee, head, as if playing a game of keep-away. *Work as a team*, the coach nearby said. *You can't leave the field until you work to-gether.* He pointed his pencil at the stud in my group. The stud intentionally dropped the juggle and passed the ball to me. I started a juggle, bouncing the ball on the tops of my cleats for a few seconds before I dropped it. Using my hand to prop the ball up, I tried again, but the same coach shouted: *No hands!* I put the ball down and passed it back to the stud. The coaches reunited in midfield, said some things, and crossed out notes on their papers.

*Forty-five seconds, boys*, both coaches barked. After a couple minutes, the other groups on the field emptied, leaving just my group, which included a chubby boy who was about as bad as I was, the stud, and me. The stud, who was the son of one of the coaches and already knew he made the team, had huffed and puffed the entire time, frustrated to be grouped with us. Every time the stud started the juggle and sent the ball our way a *come on, dude* followed, the ball dropped, another unsuccessful juggle.

It must have been painful to watch. The ball rebounded between us, off my foot or the chubby kid's foot, the juggle only lasting ten seconds or so. *Are you even trying?* the stud said louder than he intended, and then his dad walked toward us. We could hear the swish of his wind pants first. The shadow of his crossed arms hovered, just this blacked out figure that watched and waited. *Start the juggle*, he said, and then aimed his clipboard at me. I started, using my toe to prop the ball, and then centered it on my cleat to keep the tempo, *tap*, the ball floated, *tap*, and then again, *just a little harder, just take your time, just focus on the ball*, I thought, and it popped above my waist. I jolted my knee for the next step, to send it to one of my group members, but the ball ricocheted, completely missing anyone in my group. With a quick frustrated sigh, I said: *Did I do that?* and jogged for the ball.

When I returned, the stud in my group scoffed to himself, as if saying, why are you still on the field, why are you even trying out for this team, you are horrible at soccer, you're a loser. He chuckled louder, for everyone to hear, and then said what I had said, but differently, high-pitched and nasally: *Did I do that?* His laughter rose, like he was onto something and said it again. *Did I do that?*

The coach, the stud's father, sidelined us. The stud pranced to his friends, ready to tell them something. The chubby kid wasn't too bothered, like he was just glad it wasn't him under the adolescent knife of ridicule. I jogged to the sideline and looked for an empty spot away from everyone, but the bench was crowded with boys giggling like hyenas. I slumped at the end of the bench, my butt barely sticking to the aluminum, while the two boys next to me elbowed each other. My body was rounded over. And in between the chatter, who was probable to make the team and who wasn't, and only in low volume at first, just a couple kids, but then loud enough for me to hear it: *Did I do that?* with the same obnoxious emphasis on *that*, pulling the *t* comically. They gained attention, like a bullying contagion, like a lunchroom chant, like a gang of jokers, gap-toothed smiles, glints of braces, red-stained Gatorade tongues. *Did I do that? Did I do that?*

I hid my face in my shirt, pretending to dry it off. Some kid, maybe the stud or maybe not, not that it really mattered because these kids became one kid, but his voice reached higher than all of them and said: *He looks just like Steve Urkel, has the same glasses, and the annoying voice, and he's Black, too. Did I do that?*

I've been punched in the gut before; I've caved over, felt the breath leave me, but this was different—this was an emotional hurt that buried itself like a virus, like an illness and the symptom was looking different, was being Black, was being an outsider. So in that dirt-stained shirt sometime after the final whistle blew and minivans arrived and the grass had dried and our bodies cooled and those kids carried on asking *did I do that* like I was some kind of dirty joke. With my shirt still covering my face, I broke in half. I cried, and I couldn't stop.

What I couldn't understand then was that when my coaches saw me, the body of a brown boy, they saw athleticism; they saw action, something that does, that jumps higher, runs faster; they saw a body that would give them an advantage. *We'll get the win this season.* As a kid, I didn't recognize the narrative associated with my color; I only recognized the need to fit in, to be a part of the team, and that's why I was disappointed. I was left out. The coaches, in comparison, were disappointed I was not the naturally gifted ethnic athlete they'd hoped for. Instead, I was a clumsy, overanxious, rail-thin kid whose legs tangled, a boy who couldn't keep up with the soccer ball, a boy who was as un-Black as those white kids. And to them, the kids on the sidelines still holding their bellies in laughter, to them, I became nothing more than a caricature, just a parody of a person from television. They were kids from a small town with almost no people of color, a town where it really didn't matter if you thought or believed or even said that all Black people look alike.

How I wished to become the all-star Black athlete the coaches wanted, to hear those parents cheer while I drove that ball down midfield. I imagined I'd breach the defense when dribbling from foot to foot in high speed as if on fast-forward. I imagined how I'd wind my muscular leg and rocket that ball like my toe was a hot ignition, how everyone would scream *GOAL*, and the crowd would roar, and the bleachers would shake—how after that, I'd rip off my jersey and slide across the field, grass and dirt spritzing, how then they'd say *he's just like Ronaldinho.*

I didn't move like Ronaldinho, and I never would. I preferred reading books and drawing comics to running and kicking balls. I liked my cartoons on Saturdays and not watching sports. I didn't mind wearing glasses because it helped me look smarter. I knew I wasn't white but rarely thought of it. And yet, what I did want, on this soccer field, on this beautiful day, at this tryout, was to fit in. But instead, I did the complete opposite and was reminded just how different I was. That maybe I did look like Steve Urkel, that maybe we were alike, and when those kids saw me, they imagined him. They saw me running in high-rise jeans, suspenders, giant red-framed glasses, brown saddle shoes, and a cardigan, stumbling down the field. They imagined my lanky legs in some cartoonish tangle like a human pretzel. They imagined me defending two players while they lobbed the ball over my head, and, like a monkey, I'd sprawl, whoop, and jump. They imagined line driving the ball smack into my face, just to see me fumble for my glasses. And maybe in their imaginations or in real time, I'd say *did I do that* again, and someone would signal the laugh track, and those kids would roar and point fingers at the brown kid who did not make the club soccer team.

# BEFORE CELL PHONES

.........

WE shook Mom's workpants, rustled in her pockets and peeked through holes with grubby fingers. We claimed loose pennies and quarters. On our bikes, we chased down the sun that was swallowed by the frothy blue sky. Our shoelaces dragged and followed us like the loose Band-Aids swinging from our dirty knees. Our names were abbreviated to single letters and howled between belly-deep laughter and the sounds of cards taped between our tire spokes. We pedaled swiftly through the deep-wooded wilderness. With the fidelity of childhood dares, someone called: *No hands!* We were hawks cutting air with our arms. And in the afternoons when the siren screamed from the ice cream truck, we ditched our bikes, leaving them in the dirt like bones. We shook our dingy dungaree shorts, rummaged in our pockets and peeked through holes with hungry fingers. We freed a palm of pennies and quarters. We ordered the tan-colored cones—*hey, try mine*—and shared overzealous licks. And when the reluctant nightfall came, it carried us home, before the time when cell phones were pinging.

# BETWEEN WALLS AT A FRIEND'S HOUSE

.........

AND I think it's like the spaces between people, between rooms, between studs, between sheetrock, between walls, when I overheard the conversations my friend's parents had about my family, about Black people, about how there was a difference between Black people and niggers, and we were not niggers but good Black people—good Black people who were more like them and less like niggers—and how it was okay that he and I were friends, that he could go to my house, any time but never sleep over, just in case—just in case we really were what they thought we were. And while both awake, my friend and I listened and said nothing to each other, and I think he was hurt and embarrassed, and I was embarrassed to be Black and be there and be his friend. But we both wore Phat Farm and FUBU, and we both idolized Black athletes, the men taped to his bedroom walls, and I borrowed *his* rap CDs, and he knew more words to their songs than I did, and that it was just one mighty damn contradiction.

# BUT I AM NOT TOBY

.........

TIMELINES were important to Mom. *To know where you're going, you have to know where you came from.* The importance of ancestry. She'd say that most Black people don't know their history. She'd sit me down and go over a list of books: *Narrative of the Life of Frederick Douglass, From Slavery to Freedom, I Know Why the Caged Bird Sings, Things Fall Apart, Black Boy,* and *Black Like Me.* In many of our lessons, I was never interested. She could read with one eye and keep the other eye on me, waiting and waiting for my response, for me to finally say *I get it, Mom.* But I never said much, and I didn't get it. I wanted to learn in school and not at home. Mom would say things like *do you know why the caged bird sings?* With a long exhale and drop of my chest, I'd tell her no and catch my eye to somewhere else. Then Mom would say *the caged bird sings because it has to, to prove it's free.*

I didn't understand what she meant. I didn't understand freedom, or at least, not freedom like that, something involuntary. But I'd pretend to listen intently, studying the pages of the book, and let my attention drift elsewhere when she wasn't looking. Mom took on those narratives, as if Maya Angelou was some distant relative. Mom would flip the book over and show me the author photo. She'd say *look*, with dignity and pride, *that could be you*. And I would look and try to find some similarities in the author's face, something that might look like me. But I couldn't. My lips were thinner, my nose was sharper, my hair was much too curly. Maybe they looked like Mom or her family but not like me. I was Black like none of them.

.........

Mom gave me those books as a prerequisite, an instructional manual to being Black, like some necessary reading. Mom said that even though I was only half Black, one drop of the blood made me Black enough. She'd say *you need to learn about your people*. About how schools didn't teach everything about our history, that it was her job as a mother, a Black mother, to teach me.

We'd sit at the kitchen table for what felt like hours, reading and skimming through the litany of supplemental books. She'd hand me highlighters, Post-It notes, and sheets of paper. To appease her, I'd jot down random names and dates that seemed important: Booker T. Washington, 1865, Umuofia, Shaka Zulu. She'd continue on: *When Black people came to America as slaves, they were not just stripped of their freedoms but were stripped of their language, their history*. She'd tell me how slave traders would split up families and their histories and legacies were lost.

She said that's why Frederick Douglass learned to read, so he could tell our stories.

But I didn't want to tell *our* stories. I just wanted to be a teenager.

Mom would print out pixelated photos on our home printer, photos from slavery, like the blueprints of slave ships from the Middle Passage. She'd say *honey, we were the cargo.* I'd watch her finger trace where the chained slaves would be and try to feel something, to feel a sense of relevance, to feel anger, to feel sadness, but I didn't feel anything besides annoyance—I just wanted to watch television. Mom preached about my school not teaching about Africa, nothing besides the heroics of people like Abraham Lincoln and John Brown. She told me Africa was not to be defined solely by slavery—Africa was a beautiful country with kingdoms, culture, food, universities, literature, and a history—it was more than wars, poverty, famine, and AIDS. We'd read chapters from Chinua Achebe's novel, *Things Fall Apart.* We'd talk about Okonkwo's coming of age journey, and Mom would say *honey, he's stubborn, like you.* And when Mom finally closed whatever book we were reading, *The Autobiography of Malcolm X* to *From Slavery to Freedom: A History of Negro Americans*, she'd end with the same question: *Without history, who are you?* I never had an answer. I didn't know who I was, or at least, where I fit into the Black narrative.

To help me to ground my heritage, my history, she told me about her mother. *You know Nana had to move up North for many years because how bad things got in*

*Alabama. The Great Migration, honey, and everybody was trying to escape the recesses of slavery, like the Jim Crow laws.* Mom said *it got so bad that Nana's uncle was killed for doing nothing, just because he was out on a Saturday night, walking around town with no job.* She said that the police called it loitering. Then they took him into holding and booked him. Mom said he never left. The police killed him that night. She said *you should always take injustice personal.*

Mom kept stockpiling those books. When we stopped reading them together, I told her I would read them on my own, but I never did. They stayed in the dust of my teenage mess, in a drawer of old socks and forged parental signatures. Instead, I read about Harry Potter.

.........

In February, Black History Month, Mom probed me about what we were learning in school. I'd spit whatever random thing about Black History I knew, something about peanuts, the Thirteenth Amendment, and Harriet Tubman. Maybe my defiance was out of spite. In some way I was saying *Mom, I do not want to be different from my classmates*, those classmates who knew just as much about Black people as I knew or pretended to know. So, I began to hate February, especially.

As a result, my grades dropped. I kept my head down, doodled in class, tried to escape whatever lesson—go to the bathroom or just roam the halls. But eventually, I was sent to the principal's office or to the guidance counselor and was questioned about my recent decline in attitude and work ethic, a litany of: *Davon, what's going on? Did something happen at home? Did something happen in class?* But I never gave them an answer, at least not a real one. I was too embarrassed—too embarrassed to say that I did not want to be Black in a white town in February.

Whenever I got home from school on a day when someone from whichever office called, Mom would be at me again, fiercely reminding me what my people did for an equal education: *Plessy v. Ferguson* and *Brown v. Board of Education. Black people died for your future. How dare you not take advantage of what our people did for you.* To be fair, I agreed with her. I believed it was all true. But in this town with a 0.9 percent Black population and a 96 percent white population, I felt like the accidental inkblot on a blank sheet of white paper.

.........

In English class, in a reading circle discussing *To Kill a Mockingbird*, I counted each student and each paragraph to anticipate who was next to read out loud. I hoped to God it wouldn't be me. There were racial slurs in like every other sentence. I searched, as if looking for a typo, anticipating one word—*nigger*. I swear I could feel the word getting closer, as if this dorsal fin were rising from out of the pages. And then there was an irrefutable reaction toward the disyllabic sound, like an anaphylactic trigger, deep in my gut, and a titan of a thing would be released from the innermost part of me. I couldn't say it. I wouldn't say it. And though I'd try to predict who would be next to read with enough time to excuse myself to the bathroom, it seemed I could never outrun it. The damn thing smelled my blood and ate me whole every time.

Somehow it would resurface again and again and not just when specifically learning about Black people, but in other forms of academia. In Music History, we were learning about the evolution of music. We discussed a variety of the greatest musicians. We were in the '60s and '70s eras, discussing rock 'n' roll musicians like The Beach Boys, The Beatles, and the Rolling Stones. We listened to each band's most popular songs. We read their mini biographies. We learned about their influences and tried to really answer what made them so revolutionary to American music. They were movers and shakers and were still influential to that day. Our teacher said that music would continue to change with the different generations. She asked us for other examples of newer genres. We said pop, heavy metal, alternative rock, folk, techno, and rap. She agreed, but then thought for a moment and said rap was not a genre—rap was not real music. She seemed adamant about it, almost irritated someone even said it. She said rap was explicit—the lyrics were disgusting and offensive, and rappers weren't even real musicians.

It was as if she were talking straight at me, channeling years of frustration to the only Black student in class. And I wasn't even the student who mentioned rap as a genre. I knew better than to willingly turn the spotlight on myself. But that hot seat was boiling, and I slid down in my chair to try and hide behind the person in front of me. I felt that same uneasy feeling, as if my stomach were in the sea, and everyone was watching me capsize. They must have been thinking and assuming I would have some retort. Of course, I had to love rap. I had to disagree with our teacher and spring into an argument, had to fight for my people. For I was, like always, the only person of color in the classroom. And then suddenly, yet it felt premeditated, our teacher asked me directly: *Why do they say nigger so much if they hate being called niggers?*

.........

In American History when learning about Emmett Till, we saw pictures of Black bodies hanging from trees, and the crowds of people smiling and posing, as if the bloated things were sport, like big game quarries from last night's hunting: deer, elephants, elk, men. The human ugliness was full screen on the projector. While looking, I questioned myself. I questioned the overwhelming sadness I felt. Was it basic human empathy or something different—something intrinsic, like a piece of me was suspended from those trees? I thought about Mom. I imagined that man dangling from the tree on Main Street in whatever town could have been her brother or her uncle or one of her sons. I remembered Mack Parker in *Black Like Me*, and I wanted to close my eyes and look away, like always.

.........

The pinnacle of Black History Month in school was when we watched *Roots*. Our teacher rolled in the television and pulled one disc from the brick-sized DVD box. We normally felt a rush of relief to watch movies in class, like *Rudy* or *Dead Poets Society*, but this would be different.

This was not entertainment, as we often thought. It would not just be a few racial epitaphs or uncomfortable and unsettling photos or like the handful of chapters in our history book, the footnoted descriptions of shackles and the deeds to the human property. No. This was slavery, one thousand and eighty minutes of slavery, spanning a hundred years of slavery, slavery made for television, the American history of an entire race of people in eighteen sixty-minute episodes.

Before it started, I swore I'd wear my toughest skin. I wanted to be strong and brave, and I wanted to pretend it wouldn't affect me like how Mom said it would. She had told me about *Roots*, about how her family had watched its television premiere on ABC in 1977, how every night, after every episode, they all cried like someone they loved had just died. It was as if Toby, the protagonist and slave, was a son, a brother, a friend to her family. But I wouldn't let that happen to me. I couldn't. I had to keep my facade that none of this ever bothered me. That I was a participant to learning like everyone else—not the thing that was being learned. I had to prove to my classmates that I was somehow different from the people they now watched on the television screen. And after every moment, every wrong that was being done, my classmates' heads slowly turned, like an audience in a theatre, like they were looking for someone, always looking for me, as if wanting to ask: *Is this really true? Are you upset? Does the N-word offend you? I'm sorry.* And as much as I did want to cry, as much as I was offended—and I imagined every one of my Black family members being lashed and beaten and broken like the branches on the old tree that hanged more bodies than it had in rings of bark—despite that, I kept silent. But I was waiting for someone to turn and look at me, for I would grit my teeth and tell them *but I am not Toby.*

# THOUGHTS ON HAIR

.........

I remember my cousin's cornrows. I remember my aunt sitting on the couch, my cousin sitting on the floor between her knees, getting his hair braided. His head was tilted, and he winced and grimaced and said *stop*, but my aunt never did. She dipped two fingers into an oil that she used to rub on my cousin's scalp. *This'll keep your skin soft.* Half of his head was afroed, and the other half was not. And when he wiggled about, my aunt gave him a slap on the back of his neck, *sit tight boy*, and he did.

I could never understand exactly how my aunt did it. I often tried, stretching my hair in the longer spots and twisting. It never quite stuck. I tried the top of my head, by my ears, and the back, zigzagging the sprawling whirls but nothing. But my aunt crafted different designs—down the middle, parted to the sides, in big swirls. I didn't think my cousin appreciated it like I did. To me, it was artistry but to him, it was torture. After a couple days when my cousin washed out the dust and dried skin, I watched my aunt braid his hair again.

.........

*What do you want to get braids for?* My hairstylist always said while pinching the long strands of crinkly hair between her oily forefingers. This was part of our biweekly conversation, reminding me that, as she reasoned *you have good hair.* But I had reasons, each one starting with *I want to look just like so-and-so.* Whatever I said, she was never convinced. In the packed salon—all Black and brown women—with some in chairs next to mine and others under the dryer, agreed and often crowded around my hairstylist and me, complimenting my curls and taking turns running their hands in the unbraided hair. They'd say *oh, if I had hair like you.*

.........

*Oh, if I had hair like you,* I've heard more than I remember.

In in the seventh grade, all the boys in my school wanted hair like this kid, Matt, who embodied the hairstyle the Biff, named for the notorious character from *Back to the Future*, Biff Tannen. When Biffed, Matt's hair was combed straight from back to front, but the bangs were flipped up like a ski jump. In the hallways between classes, Matt was followed by a constant crowd of onlookers, both boys and girls—girls who had a crush on the hairstyle and boys who wanted to look like that. Lots of kids tried to mimic Matt's hair. One kid buzzed his entire head but left the Biff patch, just a near-bald head and a stamp of hair molded to a point with a glob of hair gel. He wasn't complimented, and he hid in the bathroom most of the time to avoid ridicule. But who could blame him? It was a fad like anything else, like when the girls in school wore scrunchies on their wrists. Our school's bathrooms were covered in excess hair gel—a thick film crusted in the sink drains, around the faucets, and coated the mirrors. After school, the custodians scrubbed off our narcissism with futile results, knowing tomorrow the gel would make its return.

I first tried to recreate the Biff by only using water. Normally, my hair was a three-inch ball of curls, and not those luscious locks seen on television ads, but more of a frizzy ball. With water, I matted the hair on the crown of my head, first using my hand and then a comb. If successful, I would tease the hair closest to my forehead into the quint-essential Biff. In the mirror staring at myself, I toyed with the hair, trying to get the curls to tame, to change—to be straighter. I finished with nothing resembling the Biff and was left with a tumbleweed mess, hair twisting and twirling in all directions like Buckwheat from *The Little Rascals*.

Convinced it wasn't the end, I begged my mom to pur-chase the hair gel everyone at school used, LA Looks, which was available in an array of colors. She agreed and took me to the drugstore where I bought a bottle of the coral-blue Extreme Sport Level 10. In the car, I read the directions: *Apply to towel-dried hair. Style as desired.* I imagined myself parading the hallways at school, everyone would be jealous, even Matt, thinking that his time as the Biff was up. Maybe I'd take his position on the soccer team. Maybe the other boys would want to look like me. Maybe my hair would finally look like theirs.

When I got home, I rushed to the bathroom, the plastic bag swinging and swishing. I doused my hair with water to make it wet, as directed, and the fuzz ball dropped an inch or so. I pulled for a towel and dried my hair. With the towel around my shoulders, I flicked and teased using a comb, and smoothed the hair into a downward slope. I squeezed the gel bottle until the blue ooze snaked into the palm of my hand, and then, with precision, I stroked the gel into my hair with four fingers. Immediately after, I loaded more gel into my palm and forked the hair above my forehead to a point. I applied another coat to the entire thing and matted the loose curls straight.

Feeling confident and knowing that tomorrow at school everyone would be jealous, I struck a pose, smiled with a mouth full of braces and a head like plaster. I wanted some affirmation that I looked as cool as I thought, so I called to my big brother for his advice. When he came in, he gave me a look, scrunching his face like he saw something odd, and said *why you want to look like a white boy?*

.........

Before I wanted hair like the Biff, I wished for hair like my brother, Troy. I'd watch him in the bathroom before school brushing his hair, using a palm brush with hard black bristles like a porcupine's back. Sometimes when he wasn't looking, I'd try his brush, but its coarse bristles hurt my scalp. He'd follow a specific course, brushing his crinkly hair in long slow strokes, moving from the front to the back, methodically, as if sanding wood. His hair took on a new form, from the tuft of a carpet to what looked like the smooth ripples of a pond. When I'd ask Troy about it, he'd tell me that he was getting *waves*, which was the style of brushing one's hair until it furled. He'd tell me not stare too much or *Davon, you'll get seasick*. I didn't know what he meant and stared and just wanted to *get waves* too.

Instead of using hair gel, Troy used Murray's Pomade. From a round tin, he'd swab only the smallest amount of pomade on a finger, and then dab it at the top of his head. He'd brush it next, buffing it until it shined. The pomade broke down into a softer substance, spreading easily as if margarine. It smelled like man or the way men were supposed to smell, like sandalwood, sawdust, and grease. To keep his *waves* secure into the next day, Troy wore one of our mom's nylon stockings on his head to bed. I thought he looked like a robber, but I still begged him to don my curly head with one of his extra stocking caps.

When Troy needed a haircut, our dad used his clipper set. With a guard attachment, the clippers easily sheared off Troy's hair like mowing a lawn. Afterward, our dad used a smaller clipper, like a protractor, and angularly shaped the front, sides, and back. But when it was my turn for a haircut, he only needed a wet comb and a pair of scissors to style and snip the twirling things off. After both haircuts, the bathroom floor was covered in tough clumps of Troy's hair and the whirls of feathery ruffles of my hair. Just like the hair on the floor, Troy and I looked so different, and I wanted us to look the same.

.........

In my high school's gym locker room, I wrapped a do-rag around my head, so my cornrows wouldn't frizz or undo. I set the base at the top of my head, wrapped two strings around my forehead twice, and then tied a small knot in the back. It looked like a silky bandana. After that, I could take off my shirt, put my gym shirt on, untie the knot, remove the do-rag, and then go to the gymnasium for class. While none of the other boys spent time adjusting their hair like I did—those boys who were white and not like me— it sometimes took me an extra five minutes, a relatively annoying process every time I had to undress and redress. But if I didn't do that, my cornrows would barely last two weeks. As my hairstylist put it *your hair is too soft to stay like this long.*

The worst part of wearing cornrows was not the daily precautions—tying the do-rag or having to wear a shower cap whenever I showered. The worst of it was the never-ending questions from my peers. Questions that teetered between curiosity and condescension. In my predominately white high school, cornrows were a wonder, a rarity. I was the only male minority student with cornrows. At that time in the early 2000s, a vast number of Black athletes, musicians, and actors had the same hairstyle: Allen Iverson, Randy Moss, Ludacris, Carmelo Anthony, Xzibit. And this might have been all they knew, my peers, all they could relate to or understand about Black men. For their experiences with Black people were nonexperiential, rather, an interpretation, as an audience of the fourth wall. So they were at me with their ignorant *you look just like* . . . And I bet the few other minority students, the Black girls who modeled ethnic hairstyles, received the same litany of side-eyes and questions: *Do you wash your hair? Is your hair dirty? Why do you tap at your hair? Can I touch it?*

Woe is me, right? But is that not what I wanted, to be noticed—to be compared to this person and that person? Because wasn't it cool to be Black if it was cool to be Black?

.........

It took almost two years to grow my hair long enough for cornrows. My aunt, who braided my cousin's hair, told me that since my hair was so straight in comparison to my cousin's, it needed to be longer. And every time I asked her to braid it, she'd say *it's just too short*. So, I waited, and it grew—fast, but not fast enough.

Troy was always teasing my *before look*, before the cornrows. He referred to it, my hair, as the Jew-Fro. He called me Albert Einstein, and I had the glasses to match. So I wore a hat whenever I could. And in school, I accepted any ridicule with proud proclamation that my cornrows were only weeks away, and I'd look just like any one of the Black men I idolized. I was dedicated, maybe more than anything I had ever dedicated myself to—dedicated not just to the hairstyle, but to the idea of it. Cornrows were a statement, something undeniably Black, something Black people owned, and with it, I would finally identify.

But I also remember when the white girls in my school came home from vacations in the Caribbean. I remember how their blonde or brown hair was tightly woven into braids. I remember seeing their pale scalps and the sounds that the colorful beads made when the girls turned their heads. I remember hearing about the relief they felt when they took the braids out, days later, now being back to normal—being back to white because being Black was just a hairdo. I remember feeling angry, but not entirely with them, but angry with myself—angry because we were the same. I was just like those girls. I was appropriating the part of Black culture that I wanted too.

The versatility of my hair has always been like wearing a mask, using a different language, being someone else, a different race, at my choosing. With a buzz cut, I'm Mexican, call me Carlos. A combed slick-back, I'm Tony, the Sicilian. The Caesar-cut and high fade, I'm the Dominican, Miguel. With a thick beard and crew cut, I can be Muhammad, the Iraqi. And with cornrows, I'm the light-skinned Black man named Malik. Names are as stereotypical as assigning hairstyles to race; and yet, it's what I've done all my life. My hair has been my identifier. It has given me false security. And I'm guilty of taking on these different cultures—guilty of this appropriation, guilty of gainfully being racially ambiguous.

# THE ANGELS OF
# THE PAINT

.........

IN those late winter months when the sun broke early and night came urgently, as if the sky were flicked on and off— in those days when we were ghosts outside and our shadows paced in the overcast of a streetlight—back then, after homework was finished and before dinner was served, you could find us on the basketball court: jump shots, lay-ups, behind-the-backs, phantoms on fast breaks in high-tops. You could find us living for the glory of fadeaway three-pointers. You could find us mimicking the sounds of a swish or the clank of a missing basket on the board. You could find us like animals on stampedes above the black asphalt, chasing the ball as if prey.

Basketball was all we thought about, all we discussed. In school and in math class, somehow a quadratic equation would better our shot. In history class, we presented biographies on Naismith and Spalding. In health class, the food pyramid started with Gatorades. In science class, any hypothesis began and ended with what would increase our vertical leaps. If we could, we'd wear our team uniform to school, but instead chose AND1 brand attire—the jersey with no sleeves, the polyester shorts below our knees, the sweatbands and wristbands, the "All Ball or Nothing" slogan. We lived for The Game. We went to war for The Game: four boys, two-on-two, fighting for one ball, one hoop, and the namesake. Hot brows and busted lips, jammed thumbs and sore wrists, momma jokes and shit talk, *screen, screen, box 'em out, that's butter, brick, snuffed, yo, run that back*, the language of our realm.

We'd spend all night out there, training for the next game—running suicides from either side of the court, dribbling with our eyes closed between cones, practicing free throws and one-twos and two-threes from out of bounds. We played until the dark exhausted the light, until the ball would undoubtedly be lost after bouncing one final time off the rim. And when that happened, which it always did and none of us volunteered to go find it, we'd turn in and look up, with our backs against the court. We'd give the stars our eyes and dream. Maybe like the Greeks did, how they dreamt of Orion and Pegasus, how they imagined the glories of their battles. While under those same stars after however many games to twenty-one—sweating, slick, cold, and wet—we dreamt of our gods, our heroes.

We dreamt of the day when we could grab rim, the day when we could lift from the ground as effortlessly as Vince Carter or Kobe Bryant. We dreamt of the clean crossovers, like Allen Iverson, leaving whatever defensive player with two broken ankles. We dreamt of buzzer-beaters, of Reggie

Miller shooting outside the three-point line with five seconds left. We dreamt of the dribblers, the free throwers, the triple-doublers, the men who flew on Nike swishes—the angels of the paint.

# SUICIDE ON THE TRIPLES

.........

WE'D rather wait for a game of four-on-four to end than play over there. Gathered around the perimeter and sitting cross-legged on the grass, we'd watch bodies bounce with the ball up and down the court. A rule passed from some kid to another, so we knew never to play on that hoop perched closest to the woods. It loomed as one does—a shadow, stretching from out of bounds to the foul line like a giant scythe. But it never deterred the games. Subtracting that hoop's half-court, at least three games could run—triple-halves or one full and one half.

Typically, it was The Triples, and that's what we called them before gathering and then departing from home on our bikes. There were some kids standing on pegs and some pedaling, a quarter mile through fetterbush, hollies, and oaks—over one rickety four-by-four and across a bridge of plywood that sat above a brook, and then walk the bikes by our sides along a two-housed property line where the kid that no one talked to lived. We imagined that he peeked out the window, watching us like Boo Radley—his face slightly smudged against the glass breathing slow and heavy and desiring. So, tight-lipped, we passed, with bikes in hand and a ball stuffed in our shirts and in our shorts: the One-Bosomed Woman, the Pregnant Baller, or Big Ball Sack Bob for the kid who could carry the most balls in his shorts.

When we got there, you could hear the clank of an off-put shot; you could hear feet and legs in a constant shuffle; you could hear a kid yelling *I got next*; you could hear twelve-year-olds speaking a language you might not understand—how *pass the rock* meant send an assist, how being *on fire* meant consecutively scoring, how *that's butter* was a perfect swish.

But you'd also see that no one played on that lone court no matter how many kids stood on standby. They wouldn't ever step on that asphalt. Rumor was you'd instantly break thumbs and sprain ankles. Rumor was the one kid who came down so hard after a rebound he tore both ACLs, and the other kid who lost two fingers in the net—how his blood sprayed red and the red-painted rim that mouthed the metal-chinked net kept those fingers, how sometimes if you looked long enough, you'd see the outline of a body still hanging.

The superstition was strong, and when the night came, how it comes in the Pine Barrens—quick, sudden, like a boundless cloud creeping and taking hold of the sky—how the trees closed, like a mouth, huge and earthy, and consuming what was left of the sun, we mounted our bikes without verbal cue—watching the light fade quickly, and those basketball hoops stood eclipsing like sundials. With no LEDs above the court, we scurried. Fear of the dark was a real thing—how the woods reached and grabbed, how the darkness was malleable, how it was as black as that asphalt. So we didn't travel those trails back home; we took the main road.

This was also when the shift changed, when the big kids arrived while we left, coming sound first, the bass and treble of their cars booming, their engines revving, trying to scare us off. We shared the hoops through fear as well as by the hour. And when their cars parked, they used high beams to spotlight the courts.

That's where they say they found him, at some shift-change, that he didn't want the children to see; that whatever day after we left and before the teenagers arrived, he strung a rope around his neck, attached it to *that* rim, and dropped and kicked and the whole hoop shifted a little and then stopped.

.........

The kid from school whose house bordered the courts and whose dad was rumored to have hanged himself from that basketball hoop never talked much, but he was large and would have been an athlete if he wanted, though he never played sports. No one ever said anything to him. We were all as scared of this giant as much as what happened to him, that this horror followed him, this death clung to his body: how he slumped in the cafeteria and classrooms, how slow and sad he walked in those hallways, how he was just like a monster. And it stunk, the death and the kid, a wet dog stench that didn't wash out. It nestled in him—in his hair, his skin, his clothes, and bones, and it never let go.

# SHOPPING WITH KRIS

.........

OUR bodies were the grit of the soil that became some self, some soul intertwined with the things here long before us. We grew from that fertile foliage, as if we were living in that tree house—that warped collage of wood rising maybe ten to twelve feet. The entire structure was rickety, and its turned-out nails were hazardous, and our idolatry, like pagans—half boy, half man, half something else—touching the space as if it were always new, as if the cigarettes, warm beers, and all else would become encyclopedias of how to step away into a world and reclaim it as ours.

Kris and I could have been pirates in some other life. Our shirts mouthing open like foresails. Our legs pumping like oars. Aboard one Schwinn and one Mongoose BMX bike, we rode on, around the culs-de-sac and through the one-ways, surveying the land and looking for our rightful conquest. We stole our supplies for the tree house from homes under construction in our neighborhood. The construction workers never seemed to notice what little we took. We weren't vandals. We didn't trash. We'd take only what was in abundance, the things they wouldn't notice.

The neighborhood was divided into two sections, Holly Bush One and Holly Bush Two. I lived in Holly Bush One, the older section comprised of single-family homes built in the late 1970s. Besides being older, the homes were smaller but sat on almost an acre of land. My house wore green shutters, egg-white siding, and a two-car garage. There were four big oak trees, holly shrubs, and shredded mulch in the front yard. In the backyard, there was a white shed, a wooden swing set, and a grill. The backyard was sectioned by what my father landscaped and what he did not. Past the swing set and shed were brush, pine needles, shrubs, oak trees, and wire compost bins. In some parts back there, the leaves were ankle height—sometimes singed or sometimes dark and wet but everything was unkempt.

While doing homework, I'd watch my father landscape the front yard. He'd say something about curbside appearance, about the impression of vitality. He'd surround all the trees and shrubs with dark mulch. He spent hours out there—raking, watering, mowing, weeding, wheelbarrowing, just his body and the yard in constant motion, giving itself and losing itself. And on any autumn day, the sun would splash its warm colors across the sky, and my father and all of the neighborhood men would bend their tired backs, and with their rakes, they'd pull the fallen life into their heavy-duty stomachs of tarps—the fathers and the life being dragged together—carrying oak leaves, pine needles, sweet seedpods, and brush from their yards as if some entrails of man and earth.

Holly Bush One had been expanding into the developing land in Holly Bush Two, where a new house was going up every other month. Kris lived in Holly Bush Two, and his house was a big single-family home with four bedrooms, three full baths, bay windows, and a large patio. And though the house was beautiful, new, and spacious, the backyard was treeless and fenced, and it lacked the isolation we needed. Rather, my backyard offered us almost an acre of removal, of detachment, of no lattice fences or white picket suburbanization. And inside us both was this irrepressibly overgrowing desire for the nature, for the woods, for the land beyond the land, for the New Jersey Pine Barrens—this place and this thing that was inside and outside of us and was growing uncontrollably like the forest itself.

The lopsided two-by-fours in the trunk of the tree had to be replaced. The planks were the stepladder to our tree house, but the wood was cracking in half because too much moisture and not enough sun caused the wood to rot. Our beloved tree house grew a thick wet and slick black skin. The constant swelling made the wood spongy and ineffective for building. It was dangerous, dangerous because of cause and effect—the dampened wood caused a nail to protrude, and Kris cut his shin on that nailhead. This was our learning, result and consequence—no scientific method or the advice from our always-omniscient parents playing loudly on the speakers of our subconscious. Our learning was always an experience.

Kris and I hid in the brush adjacent to an under-construction home. Scratching the pine needles off our ankles, we

looked both ways, our heads like periscopes. We checked
the Tyvek house wrap, the turned-up ground, the reflective
vests, and sometime after four, when the men clocked out,
and they collected their materials and dropped tool sets in
truck beds and piled themselves in truck cabs and drove out
the same tire treads they came in on, we waited till the coast
was clear—minivans garaged, dads not home—and we
crossed that street, like the Atlantic—justifiably, as if early
countrymen, manifest destiny, divine conquering, everything American—and entered that house.

Fortunately for us, the lockboxes hadn't been installed
yet—nor the deadbolt lock—only leaving the doorknobs
locked with a key to keep us out. So, I wiggled and wormed
my skinny wrist through the deadbolt hole and unlocked
the door from the inside. Opening the solid wood door,
clouds of sawdust traced the sun's slow cast across the
soon-to-be floor. Everything was silent. Maybe the fresh
nails were still vibrating, but we heard nothing and just
saw—saw the snake-shaped outlines from the extension
cords, the empty paper coffee cups, the stacks of particu-
late masks, and the fiberglass insulations that decorated the
space like giant cotton candy spindles. And then there was
us, larcenist, leaving our Airwalk sneaker footprints in the
taupe-colored dust.

The only thing keeping us from falling to our untimely
deaths through the framing wood and into the foundation of the home were thin slabs of plywood that dimpled
as we walked. They sat horizontally over the beam joists.
Every step was measured by the foot before it—heel-and-
toe, heel-and-toe—almost counting in between breaths. We

tried to map out our course on the beams themselves. At some point, there should have been fear—a lightness of the stomach, a cold sweat, a misguided step—some uncertainty, but we were fearless, were bandits with such poise, calculation, and bravado. Without speaking, we nodded *look over there* and *can we carry that*. We sized up the building supplies with one quick glance, knew what we could take, what we needed, and if we could carry it back home. And thinking now, maybe Kris and I were always this one step away from descending into a world below ours.

We were vagabonds when we stumbled out, weary-eyed, sun-stung, as if we had just woken up, sneezing out fiberglass and coughing up sawdust. Piling planks between ear and shoulder, stuffing our front and back pockets with collated coils of framing nails, our necks red, splintered, hot, our legs scratched and bleeding, we hurried from the scene of the crime. This wasn't a matter of excitement and danger—about just breaking the law for the fun of it, just to steal things—rather, this was about exploring and creating, about making our own by the taking, the pirating of life, whenever we could, with whatever we could.

We were sweaty, like the sun had just spit us out—these two fugitive boys moving through the neighborhood. We assessed our surroundings, waited for cars to pass, ducked and used ferns for cover. The wood and nails felt sharper. Our skin was clammy, or bleeding, or we didn't care enough to stop and find out. We just hustled through the deep thicket of pines and fetterbush. We just kept moving, almost to the backyard of my house. And then we heard it—sirens like birds above the tops of trees. And then we saw it—whirling flashes that turned everything red, blue, and a frightening purple. Our stomachs dropped and so did our supplies.

Something in the soil pulled us closer, like it already knew and wanted us safe, and had all these millipede arms drawing us in, sinking past the sand and the sediment and probably fossils of some old boys who hid there just the same. These moments felt scripted, like a reenactment of a Western robbery—two bandits, a bag of gold coins, and the law on our tails. I could draw my eyes and my hat down real low, say something smooth, like *you and whose army.*

And then the patrol car drove by, and we held our breath and counted the seconds. Our bodies might have twined and rooted and became part of the earth, and under our arms and between our legs, moss might have formed, and our eyes could have been green and leafy and even stemmed from the brush of our faces, and while our bones grew rings and our skin became bark, the fear in our bellies felt magnificent.

# THE JUMPS

.........

AND the right-hand turn out of our suburban neighborhood, where the houses hid behind long driveways and were safe beyond the oaks and the pines and the maples and the doors that were never locked, and my house was his house and his house was my house and our house, and we were all like brothers, but that's not the point, because after that, passing someone's red mailbox, a blue minivan, a black SUV, and a double-quad pickup truck—where the asphalt was no longer asphalt, and the grass grew like how moss is said to grow—we rode on into the back trails that some kid, whoever he was, built long ago, built as if giving us a secret, a special entrance into the Pine Barrens, like a key—*quick, under there*—the lone streetlight with some tattered Chuck Taylors wrapped around and our sign on the map that said *enter here, but beware, the earth will swallow you up*, will break your skin, kink your bike, demand your blood, and beware the deer tick, and the wolf spider, and the poison ivy, and the chigger bites, and *watch where you pee*, where you sit, where you

wander, because there are some boys out there, dangerous boys—boys who take off their shirts, who run from
your doorbells, who trample your flowers, who swing at
the pinecones, who spit up in the air—boys that bark, boys
that howl at the moon—boys that smell like the sweat of a
forest, like balsam, underarms, and cider—boys that were
us, and that place is where we grew—where we returned
after school, after a fight with Mom, or a breakup, a bad
test grade—where we gathered on our bikes, an extension
of our bones, maybe one on the back pegs or balancing
butts on handlebars or just two feet pedaling as if in a
stampede, looking and waiting to hit uncertainty, to spring
off the dirt mounds—what we called The Jumps and what
we needed and what we lived for—and when we did, like a
band of motocross bikers, when we found our front wheel
aligned on one of those masses of rounded ground, we flew,
our shadows cascaded, some sudden wings sprouted, and
we shared those pieces of sky.

# NOT THE WORST OF BOYS

.........

BEING thirteen meant a lot of things. For the first time in our lives, my friend Aaron and I were not considered children. We were teens and being a teen came with new freedoms, like a badge of jurisdiction—the extension of curfew, of responsibilities, of our place and position in the world. Aaron's parents were going on their annual trip to the Florida Keys, which meant an open house. Aaron's sister would housesit. But this year, she promised us one night of no supervision. She gave us a list of *what not to dos*, and we accepted and promised to be good and if we weren't exactly good, we'd be safe, at least.

.........

The sun was heavy, and night reluctantly draped across the billowing sky like how a mind draws itself into sleep. Aaron and I slowly pumped our legs, pedaling our bikes in circles, discussing the plan, while slinking through the outskirts of adjacent neighborhoods to assemble our crew.

First was Eric, then Kris, and last, Sam. Eric was in charge of music. Kris was in charge of snacks. Sam was in charge of getting girls. We gathered, and pedaled on, under the growth of the Pine Barrens, bobbling through the thicket. The wind blew and stretched branches, and their long finger-leaves touched like how us kids used to play tag. The umbilical strength of childhood could only stretch so far. Our JanSport book bags, colorful and stickered and stuffed with pillows and sleeping bags and hard candies, were also filled with cigarettes and beer. Pedaling into some adult world, we felt the same way—little by little, the old elementary games and songs about ducks and geese were becoming eulogies of a past quickly to be forgotten.

.........

Trying not to cough, each girl smiled in an attempt to still look cute while smoking. They perched the cigarette in their mouths like Holly Golightly. Smoking my cigarette, which was really Kris's mom's cigarette, I tried to blow little donut rings to impress them. The billows were not very round and floated flat. Eric and Sam were fetching beers from an outside cooler for the eight of us. We had already arranged who was going to hook up with who: Ariel and me, Eric and Mary, Sam and Laura, and Aaron had Jessica. Kris was the odd man out. With no girl to impress, he curled up on the couch to sulk and watch television. There was a rigid ownership in the way we *had* these girls like a contract the girls signed before coming over.

After the cigarettes died out, Eric popped a CD he'd brought into Aaron's parents' home theatre system. This was another of his mixes, a hip-hop one. Eric pressed play and turned the volume dial. The bass boomed, and Eric adjusted more dials to try and balance the sound. It didn't change much, but Eric stepped back, pleased. He nodded his head to the drumbeat and said something, but we couldn't hear him. We were all separated, by boys and girls, on the couches. We anticipated who would dance first, like how we stood on the wall at school dances. *You go first, dude*, Eric to Aaron. *No, you start*, from me to Sam. The music, a rap song about dancing in a dance club, instructed us how to bump and grind our bodies like cogs and gears, how to bend and blend our bodies like Play-Doh creations, how our bodies could collide and collage, how much fun it would be if we just listened and followed the steps. But still, no one moved in fear of looking as awkward as we looked when square dancing in gym class.

Being an adolescent was awkward in itself, especially our appearances. Our bodies were finding themselves, still growing and changing. I was scrawny with long arms and legs but a small torso. Sam was like a klutzy clown falling over his oversized feet. Eric still looked ten and had ears like airplane rudders. Kris was chubby and short like a bowling pin. Aaron looked the oldest and had something of a goatee made of about fifteen hairs that really looked like buttery breadcrumbs. None of us were really safe. We all had some pubertal quality we were struggling with. The girls too, though we didn't recognize that. Girls were just these foreign things to us, things we idolized and wanted to understand.

We all watched Jessica the most, though she sat quietly

with the other girls and tried to avoid attention. She was tallest and looked different than her friends. Her legs were ostrich long, her hands almost ruler-length, her braces wrapped about her jaw like some train on a mountain of crooked teeth, but Jessica was the only girl in our grade with breasts, and not breasts in the sense of anatomy, but breasts like some spectacle, like a giant house or the world's largest rollercoaster. She was very self-conscious and always wore loose clothing to hide her body. And even through her youthful dysmorphia, all the boys wanted to date her. Jessica took one step into adulthood, wiggled her foot, and turned back around to find us gawking. Like a hunkered bird, slouched in a baggy T-shirt, Jessica now drank her beer while we watched as poachers watch game between cross hairs. We might not have realized it then, but we were the creepy boys that girls complained about, the type of boys girls' parents warned them of, the boys who became something else, something bad when together.

.........

We couldn't quite hear each other talk, so Eric stopped the CD. The last song had been about being too hot to wear clothes. With a small collection of beers and ciga-rette butts, nothing had changed much besides one girl and one boy were elsewhere. Ariel, Laura, and Mary sat on the couch, completely uninterested in Sam, Eric, Kris, or me. Eric handed me a beer, turned to face me and not the girls and split his fingers in two and then snaked his tongue between them. *Gross, dude.* I laughed and popped the tab on my beer. *Want another one,* Eric turned back to the girls and asked. They declined. *Whatever, another one for me*. Eric pulled another beer from the cooler by the screen door. *Cheers, dude*. We struck beers, and foam frothed.

The girls were disinterested and ready to walk home, whispering to each other, shaking their heads, peering at one of their pink and floral wristwatches. *Where's Jessica?* asked Ariel, with an impatient tone, sort of like the tone Ariel would take when saying *no* if one of us asked her to dance. Laura and Mary peered around. *Where is she?* Ariel demanded more than she questioned. We knew where Jessica was but wanted to annoy them, for we'd accepted our chances of dancing or even remotely flirting with any of the girls to be over. Kris and Eric shook their heads, snickered and drank their beers. Sam grinned, his braces glinted, and shrugged. I told Ariel I didn't know either, and then we all broke into laughter. But all of us boys knew Jessica was upstairs in Aaron's parents' bedroom, like he had planned. Ariel stood. *I'm going to find her.*

Ariel went upstairs and heard Jessica and Aaron in his parents' bedroom while the rest of us shadowed behind her outside the door, which was locked. Ariel knocked, and no one answered. She knocked harder and said she and the girls were ready to leave. Still, no one answered. She knocked again, and when Jessica finally responded, her voice sounded far off and was slurred. *Go ahead*, her voice paused, *without me*. Ariel frowned, knocked again, and Jessica said *I'll be home. Aaron will walk me back.* There was a giggle from Jessica and some commotion on the other side of the door. Frustrated, Ariel scurried past all of us back down the stairs, and Laura and Mary tagged behind like mice. The girls grabbed their sparkly and studded purses and left. But we tiptoed to the bedroom door, knocked, chuckled, and someone said *do it.*

.........

Maybe a half hour since I had last been upstairs, I went up to pee and found Aaron in the bathroom washing his shirt in the sink. He was covered in a greenish yellow mess. *She puked on me, dude.* He washed his hands, fumbled in the cabinet for mouthwash, found it, gargled it, then spit. *I think she's real sick.*

In the bedroom, Jessica looked ghostly. She sat on the floor and mumbled and drooled. Aaron had propped her up on a dresser—her arms long-stretched, her shirt damp with vomit. Aaron's voice rushing, stumbling over itself, telling me Jessica started shaking and coughing until she threw up. His blue eyes were the sails of a ship capsizing. He shook his head. *Dude, nothing even happened. We just kissed some and then, puke. We gotta get her outa here.* I nodded and stepped in front of her. *Let's lift her,* he said and sunk his hands under her arms. I grabbed her feet. We lifted on three. When we did, her inert body collapsed back to the floor.

We tried to wake her up—said her name, shook her shoulders, even lightly slapped her face, but Jessica was unconscious, frighteningly inanimate, like a marionette without strings. Her head bobbed, and her face was covered by draping hair. Still in his parents' bedroom, Aaron paced. I thought we should try to get her into the kitchen, give her water, crackers. *I don't know*, I said but knew we needed to do something.

Reluctantly, we called for the other boys, who waddled in clearly drunk and giddy until they saw her. They stiffened, corpse-like. We wanted them to help us carry Jessica out of the room. I grabbed her feet and pointed for Aaron to get behind her, and he saddled under her arms again. Sam took one of her feet from me. Kris swigged the beer in his hand. Eric stood rigid.

Half dragging and half carrying, we lugged her into the hallway. But once again, she was falling out of our grips. We attempted to reposition ourselves and adjusted our hands like the arms of a stretcher. Aaron couldn't position in time, and—*thud*—we dropped her on the floor. *She's dead, she's dead*, Eric panicked. Aaron kneeled and placed his head to her chest, listening for a heartbeat. *She's breathing. Chill.* Eric couldn't chill and could barely catch his breath—*what, what if she like, dies*, he said in a stutter. *What if we go to jail*, he said louder. We all thought the same thing, studying the panic in each other's eyes.

Aaron and I grabbed Jessica again. I gripped her feet; Aaron clenched her hands. We struggled, and her body stretched like a hammock. We carried her into the kitchen while the other boys absently watched. Slowly, we eased her down, but she was dead weight and plopped onto the linoleum floor. Lying flat on her back, Jessica started retching. I thought she'd choke on her vomit—I saw that once in a movie. *Get her, get her.* I found new determination, and I hugged around Jessica's waist, and Aaron and I sat her up.

We balanced her against the bottom of a wooden cabinet. Neither of us really had any idea what we were doing.

Against the cabinet doors, she continued retching until vomit slowly dripped from a corner of her mouth. We could hear her stomach churn and her throat retch in preparation to regurgitate again. I was afraid she'd choke on her tongue, something I thought happened to people when they were drunk, like Jimi Hendrix. So I put my hand in her mouth and tried to pull at her tongue that oddly didn't fight back like a fish does—it just sat, slippery but still. Her stomach started stirring again. She retched more, and then an oozing sludge of different colors came out of her mouth. Aaron pulled a dish towel from a drawer and ran it under the faucet. We took turns wiping her mouth.

We left her there after she stopped retching and puking. The glittery glint of her eyeshadow smeared like ash across her face.

.........

We discussed how we were going to carry her to a wooded opening halfway between Aaron's house and Ariel's house. We agreed on a plan. The four of us could trudge her out, look for a place to leave her, and tell the girls after where to find her. We'd have to do it soundlessly, knowing what we were doing was wrong. We weren't the worst of boys, but we weren't the best. And under the cover of night, we knew we'd be safe. No one would call the cops or any parents because they wouldn't see us or hear us.

But before we could leave, Ariel and the girls kept calling the house phone, yelling and pleading. Every time we'd hang up the phone before they could really say anything. When the girls called yet again, we coiled the phone cord around our necks and pretended to gag. We elbowed and squeezed our bird-chests. We licked our lips, and we wiggled our tongues maniacally.

# 5-SERIES BMW

.........

DAD under the hood of his blue BMW pointed to ceramic brake pads, his finger snaked in a black latex glove. On an unfolded cardboard box, the pads had left a smudge of dust and caliper grease like metallic paw prints. Dad said *those over there might not fit.* The garage was cold, and I kept my hands in my pockets. I was learning how to be a man. Dad never went to the auto repair shop. He said *cars are like women. They never work like they're supposed to. They don't come with manuals. Even if you put their parts in all the right places, they'll still complain.* He banged on something under the hood, and then he rolled backward on the flat wheeled creeper and jabbed his oily finger into a hole made with his other hand, a crude gesture. We laughed. He said *my first car was like my first girlfriend, round and hatchback like the beat-up Datsun that kept getting rear-ended.* Dad asked for a screwdriver. *I used a screwdriver to start her up.*

# A BACK SEAT AND
# A FIRE PIT

.........

OUR knees were metronomes tapping the air, and our fingers were drumbeats against back seats, and our elbows drove into each other's soft stomach tissue, and whoever farted first would have to grab the door handle before the others balled their fists and punched legs, and the designated driver—the one who checked his rearview and side mirrors every sixty seconds and who also vowed on his life to his parents after borrowing their car that he wouldn't have a sip of alcohol—didn't have a sip of alcohol, but the three of us were drunken wild dogs howling at the moon, and in the back seat of his parents' sedan, we passed and swigged a bottle of Jack Daniel's and a warm Coca-Cola, and this was the place before the place, before arriving at fire pit parties—the place, where teenagers by the dozens, in our parents' cars and trucks, parked in the deep forgotten woods, the place where John McPhee said *the Pine Barrens are dark backlands*, Hog Hollow, Wharton Tract,

Indian Mills—and here is where we hid, where we found ourselves lost, and after steering off into the night from the asphalt with no pavement markers or street signs or street-lights or cell phone service, we tunneled into that fire pit party, however many uncharted and undeveloped acres of pineland, and we idled our cars and blared our music, and no one could hear us, and while the fire grew, the embers licking the wood planks and splitting what once was whole, we, like those embers, slipped and disappeared, and the thousands of stars above us that tried to keep watch could no longer see us.

# MORNING NOISE

.........

DAD got ready for work. It was three a.m., always three a.m. He shaved brown hairs into a lemon-scented froth. Dad nicked his neck and blotted spots of red on cotton balls that swelled with blood. Blue flakes of silver moon slid through the folds in the bathroom blinds. The hot water steamed, and his callused fingertips softened. He used a towel to wipe the froth, sheered hairs, and blood. It was Mom's towel, and he kept his face there.

But now outside the bathroom, Dad's jungle-green eyes glowed while watching her sleep. It was almost silent—only her breathing, her body rising and falling while cocooned in a blanket and his watching. Dad's uniform was already on, blue, clean, and still smelling like gasoline. He kneeled and tightened his high-ankle boot strings and walked out on the tips of his toes.

Dad got ready for work, and I searched for my house key. My eyes blinked like a blur of bulbs. I burped, shifted my weight, and straightened my back. I staggered like a bulky leaf lapping and whirling. I was drunk and winded.

I stamped my feet and wiggled my heels out of my shoes. I barely stood.

When finally I opened the back door, the pale light from what was left of the moon split our faces in two. Dad sat at the kitchen table—his shoulders stiff and taut as he rippled a spoon in his coffee. He sat like rebar, concreted by years of these three a.m. mornings. His coarse tanned skin the husk of a coconut. He stood and watched me stumble into the kitchen. He said nothing, and our bodies, like the sun and the moon, moved past each other.

# QUITTING MEANT BACK TO BABYSITTING

.........

IT was my first day of work. Kris and I parked in front of a white van with an ant logo on the side door: *Extermination INC.*—"Pest Control, Renovations, and Relocation, and Management of Pesticides"—and I was nervous because I had only exterminated with the sole of my shoe. But now I was wearing work boots.

A dog's bark rang out from the house. It startled me, and I hesitated to walk up the next step. Kris, who got me the job, laughed and gave me a nudge. *Just be cool, dude.* It wasn't that I didn't like dogs, my mom just never let us keep pets. I felt like this dog and any other domesticated animal could tell and somehow judged me because of it. Maybe the dog thought *if I'm going to bite anyone, it's going to be him.* And then I thought of the English mastiff from *Sandlot*, Hercules. I imagined this dog inside the house to be as big and frothy and ravenous. And that made me want to run, to tighten up my skin and shoes and trail away.

Kris had been working there for over a month and been bragging about it, about all the money he was making and all the really cool sounding pesticide sprays, and about how one time he wrestled down a snake. Regardless if any of what he said was true, I was a fish on the hook. Everyone we knew had a job. It was the summer when all my friends from high school were busy scooping ice cream and mowing lawns and lifeguarding—busy taking two big steps into adulthood, while I watched cartoons with a six-year-old.

Days before, my mom gave me shit for taking the job. She told me I had a responsibility to our family. She told me that my siblings had to babysit me when I was little whether they wanted to or not. She told me how my sister gave up her summers to help the family. But whenever she went on explaining things, I pretended I didn't understand. I thought somehow that my experiences were and should be different than my sister's—that I should be treated differently because when I was younger, my parents made less money and couldn't always afford daycare or a babysitter. But now, things were different. We lived in a house unlike the small apartment before moving to South Jersey. Mom and Dad, though they worked a lot, had good jobs, and there were no reasons that we could afford a Mercedes-Benz but not a babysitter. But still, I knew it was wrong for me to take the job. I knew I needed to help at home. Mom was a full-time student and working a full-time job. Dad worked from four in the morning till six in the evening. They needed the help because it was the right thing to do. Mom said if she had any extra money—and I know she did—she said she wouldn't send my little brother to daycare while in her words *you're living free and fed well and still under the rules of my home, you have no right to complain*. But I was seventeen, and I knew everything. So, we sat at the kitchen table and argued until our cheeks blued.

.........

When the door opened, two women greeted us. One woman, tall, with cropped dark hair, Dickies, and knee-high rubber boots said *I'm Jana and that's Susan*. Jana reached out for my hand. The other woman, Susan, a bit shorter and with shoulder-length brown hair and jean overalls and the same kind of rubber boots, held the dog back. I shook Jana's hand. The shake was strong, her thick fingers wrapped around my knuckles easily. Then the dog tugged at my shorts, and Susan jerked his collar. I was painfully uncomfortable, squirming like I had to pee. Inspecting me, Jana asked *you eighteen yet?* I shook my head no. *I'm still seventeen.* She gave me a look of disapproval and gave the same look to Kris. She said *you have to be eighteen to handle the pesticide sprays*. Shit. I didn't get the job. My face sank like I dropped an ice cream cone. Susan patted the dog on his head and gave me a hopeful smile. *Don't worry. We can still use you. Tour?* She attached the dog to a leash, reached into her pocket, and gave him a treat.

The front of the house had a large concrete wall blocking a busy street; it felt like being in a compound because of the sheer bulk of the property. Facing a wide wraparound stone driveway, my car was parked nearest the entrance. Closest to the house were two white vans. *Those are the work vans*, Susan said. *They're loaded with the pesticide sprays and traps.* She pointed toward the garage to a heavy-duty truck. *See those hay bales? Later, you'll unload them and take them to the horse stalls.* I nodded confidently, trying to take it all in, but I was anxious knowing I really knew nothing about what she was saying.

Jana and Kris joined us outside while we looked over the front exterior. Jana looked pensive, checked the time on her wristwatch, and said: *You have five minutes to take the ladders off one of the vans and put them back on the van without asking any questions. Do not scratch the paint. Make sure you securely detach and reattach the ladders to the carrier racks. Kris, you've done this before, but you have to show Davon how to do it.* She set her watch.

Prior to that moment, I'd been convinced I was capable of manual labor. Dad often forced me to rake leaves, shovel snow, clean the gutters, and work on his car. And he'd explain the importance of being handy, being a man. But I was always painfully reluctant, thinking I'd much rather play video games, watch television, play basketball, lift weights, or draw comics. So, when working on something, he'd be on me, saying how I wasn't doing whatever I was doing right, like always passing him the wrong wrench. I tried to follow his directions, though he'd quickly get frustrated with me, barking *I'll just do it myself,* and after sending me back inside, he would do it himself. But it wasn't that I was lazy. I just didn't enjoy it like he did. He loved mowing the lawn, fixing the shutters, repairing anything and everything. I just couldn't find that same joy. And I'd think how it wasn't my fault Mom bought me paints and an easel instead of a Tonka tool set.

.........

"Swingin' the Alphabet" should have been playing while Kris and I were two bumbling fools—tripping over our feet and getting our fingers stuck in the ladder's rungs, the flipper and spring kept unhinging, and the rope and pulley tangled—and we cursed at each other. Jana, Susan, and the dog watched, and I swore the dog was judging us too, smiling, his upright ears suddenly more upright, his tail wagging happily, saying in some dog code that I was an idiot. I don't know how long it took us, but I remember the sounds of Jana's watch telling us the time was up. Eventually though, we got those ladders planted on the van, and I was winded looking at the finished product.

Afterward, Jana and Kris had to leave for a job. I was to stay with Susan since I wasn't eighteen and couldn't legally handle the pesticides—there was more than enough work for me to do on the property, Jana said. Kris shrugged, and mouthed *sorry, dude*. They got in the van with the ladders on it and left. I was so pissed. The entire time I was under the impression that Kris and I would be working together, like he said. I had created a scenario in my head: Kris and I would be exterminators, but like Egon and Venkman, using proton backpacks to spray down critters and rodents.

.........

My first task was to unload the hay bales from the truck bed. It seemed easy enough. I lifted weights on a shoddy-looking home gym in my basement. I figured I was strong enough. And my plan was to lift a bale over my head, carry it between my shoulder and neck, and march toward the stalls to drop each one with my forklift arms like a Texas wrangler.

I pulled one bale from the truck bed, grabbing it by plastic strings with a good grip. It felt like I should have been wearing gloves. When I pulled harder to move the large thing, the plastic strings drew tighter and dug into my palms. It hurt. I thought of Dad doing his best impression of Arnold Schwarzenegger, calling me a girly-man. I knew Susan was watching, probably thinking the same thing, evaluating me, sensing just how weak I was. So I kept at it without complaint, not caring if it hurt, or even if I was doing it right, and then the bale wobbled some, inch by inch.

Finally, the bale dropped heavily off the truck bed down to the ground. I lifted the bale with my back bent, and pain shot up my body. The bale fell out my hands, and I felt like an old man in one of those commercials who croaks about back pain, about how he can't even lift his grandkids without taking five Advils. So I tried again. I was young and strong. But the same thing happened. Susan, about ten feet away, walked to me, still with the dog, in what had to be frustration. *Lift with your legs*, she said, and then she squatted, grabbed the plastic strings, and seemingly effortlessly lifted the bale, propped it close to her hips. She took little steps, keeping the bale against her body. *One foot after another, see.*

After about two hundred feet, she bent her legs and dropped the bale in front of a faded red fence. *We'll stack them here.* We walked back to the truck to get more bales. Susan pulled a bale off and showed me again how to do it. It felt strange, watching a woman being so much stronger than me—watching a woman doing the things I imagined only men could do. Mom refused to ever rake the leaves or even carry the groceries. It wasn't that I assumed women were not physically strong, I just never thought I'd be learning how to be a man from a woman.

On the third attempt, it became easier, and on the fourth, I did it without direction and demonstration. I stamped my boots in the gravel, got a wide base, placed the bale on my upper thighs, stood up, and it lifted with much more ease. Keeping the bale close to my body, I let my legs do the work.

.........

On another day, Susan, Jana, and Kris were all required to go on a job together. Jana gave me a list of to dos. She was not as warm as Susan and was less explanatory. She expected me to get it without any reiteration. I followed her outside the stone wall between the property and the street. Jana directed me, as if marshaling an aircraft, to a plot of yard between the curb and the wall, about a few feet in width, stretching the entire length of the front property. *You're going to use the tools we left out in the garage. You need to clear all these weeds.* She pointed from the mail-box to the end of the stone wall. *You'll wheelbarrow the weeds from here to compost heaps on the side of the house.* I nodded, trying to retain all that she said.

I was motivated when I stacked the flat shovel, the handheld garden hoe, and the pair of utility gloves into the wheelbarrow. And then I pushed it out into the sun that was hot and heavy and stretched panoramically like an egg had cracked and opened in the sky. It was late June and almost a hundred degrees. I began my work, follow-ing Jana's explicit directions: pull weeds, use shovel and hoe, don't completely dig holes, rip the roots, put weeds in wheelbarrow, take to compost, drop in compost, and repeat. Cars and trucks drove by leaving blurs, fumes, and the occasional honk. I wondered what people thought, passing me by, with my bent back and my furrowed brow and my brown skin. Cliché and all.

I think Jana and Susan were just finding random tasks for me to do. No one was watching my every step. I lis-tened to my iPod, worked at my own pace. I thought about Mom. If she was still angry with me. Since I started work, she and I weren't talking much. She'd ask me about my day, and as vaguely as possible, I replied to every word with *stuff* or *thing.*

.........

Payday. I felt like that dog waiting for a handful of treats, salivating at the idea of having my own money. But before I could buy anything else, I needed gas for my car since it had been below a quarter tank for at least two days. I refused to ask Mom for gas money. She always micromanaged my whereabouts—*You need to fill up again? Where were you?* And even if I had asked her, whatever extra money she had, she was using to pay her stay-at-home friend to babysit my little brother. Mom's friend offered to do it for free, but Mom had too much pride. Of course, when I babysat, she didn't pay me a dime. She'd say that no one paid her to be a mother. So it would be the gas tank first.

Today, Kris and I were working together. Jana and Susan had an appointment to schedule a big job. Besides that, we received no other information. We were to finish installing a mesh wire fence around the horse enclosure. Jana directed us to the barn, and Susan led the horses into their stalls. Watching, I was totally intimidated. I had never seen a horse that close up. Each horse was a giant beast: black hair, long strong fibrous legs, every muscle etched perfectly onto their bodies, like some Greek statue. I just kind of stared in amazement, comparing my skin and bones.

Jana and Susan set specific rules for working with the horses. Mostly it was *stay away from the horses*. Susan said it in a way that made me nervous. Then Jana continued, but not about the horses: *We have a big job coming up. That's really why we hired you both. We're going to finalize the paperwork. We're going to up your pay but also up your hours.* Of course, Kris and I were entranced by the thought of more money. Jana motioned with her hands, both thumbs together, moving like two wings, and she said *there will be bats*.

It was hard for us to do much work without discussing and speculating about the new job that involved bats. The

mesh wire for the fence was in a huge woven bundle, about
fifty inches high. Kris dragged it through the dirt. He had
helped install a portion of the new fencing before, so I followed his lead. We wore thick utility gloves, but only one
glove each. Kris, because of seniority, wore the right and
I wore the left. The bundle had to be unwound, fitted on
a wooden post, and then hammered in two spots, using
U-shaped barbed staples. Kris demonstrated first, explaining that was how Jana showed him. I agreed because what
the hell else did I know. *I wonder what they meant by bats,
like you think we'll catch them? How the hell do you even
catch a bat?* I helped Kris prop the bundle up. Kris, with
the same wonder and excitement: *Dude, we'll use little bat
traps, like nets that shoot from a gun.*

We rolled and stapled, and rolled and stapled. I flattened
my thumb a couple times with the hammer, but I was still
impressed with my workmanship. I was excited to go home
and tell Dad that I built a fence—that he'd be proud. After
what seemed like a solid hour of hard work, we stepped
back to evaluate our installation.

Jana and Susan weren't gone for long, about two hours.
When they returned, we were up to nothing much, kicking stones and talking shit. But when we heard the truck
rev, we rushed around looking busy. Jana called us to the
front of the house. Looking back at the fence, I was worried: it dimpled and sagged in the middle, which I imagined
was probably bad. Dad was always telling me *if you're not
gonna do it right, don't do it at all*, and the fence did not
look right, although Kris seemed pleased. And really for
the past week, I couldn't tell if I ever did anything correctly.

Jana and Susan just moved me from one project to the next.

The four of us went inside. Jana sat us down at the table where she flipped through different colored papers on a clipboard. *The new job is in Trenton at an old church. There's been years of bat infestations and debris in the attic, which is now causing the ceiling to collapse. We have to clean the attic and replace the insulation and the drop-ceiling and get rid of the bats.* Jana, with her clipboard, un-raveled sheets of paper. *We're starting Monday. We'll meet here, and then you guys will follow us in the van. Davon, you drive.*

When I got home, I had a full tank of gas and two hundred and thirty dollars in my pocket. I counted it five times, and my eyes were green. I told Mom about the job at the church, and how I would be driving the work van. I was damn proud, feeling useful. But Mom told me I shouldn't be driving any of their vehicles, that I wasn't insured. *Suppose something happens. Who's going to pay for it?* She never could find the positive side. She couldn't see just how independent I was. I told her I got paid, and she reminded me that I was being paid under the table, so I wasn't paying taxes. She told me to keep a record, just in case—and just in case, I waited until she turned around for my middle finger to show her how I felt.

.........

A thirty-minute drive, and I was nervous the whole way, gluing my hands at three and nine. After every bump, it sounded like something in the back broke or sprung off a hook. Kris reminded me the rear doors were locked, and two bungee cords wrapped around the handles for extra security. I double-checked my mirrors, stopped at yellow lights, and stayed under forty-five miles per hour in the right-hand lane.

The church looked like a small preschool building, but with a large steeple reaching about fifty feet. The whole thing was a faded color, maybe taupe or what used to be white. There was a sign out front that said "Methodist and Under Construction." We walked in, through the aisles, around the pews, and up to the altar. It was empty and kind of eerie, like horror movie eerie, postapocalyptic, with holes in the ceiling, debris, cardboard, paper shreds, loose change, broken glass, and no signs of people. Jana told us the church was over sixty years old, and the bats had infested the attic years back. It was obviously so bad that the church had to be closed until the bats were removed and everything was replaced and repaired.

Kris and I were sent to the attic. To get to there, we had to go through a sub attic, kind of like a small crawl space, less than a hundred square feet. We couldn't stand, so we hunched, trying not to bump our heads. The sun hit the stained glass inside the room making it like one big kaleidoscope—every couple minutes, the room appeared to change, and the sun created a new design across the drywall—oceanic blue, tomato red, blood orange, a prism.

Since the ceiling was low, there was no need for a ladder to get into the attic proper. We moved a flimsy strip of wood that covered the entrance, stood, and were in the attic. Heat and musk poured out. *You first, dude*, Kris suggested. I was hesitant too. I wouldn't say I was afraid of the dark, but I wouldn't say that I liked being in the dark. We were equipped with LED flashlight headbands, so I hit the switch before popping my head up. *I'm going in.*

Dad used to tell me when he was a kid living in Panama, he saw bats all the time. He said how giant they were and were known to drink the blood right out of little monkeys that he called titi monkeys. He heard the titi monkeys would be left bone-dry in the blackness of night, and he even saw the little skeletons hanging from the trees. Dad said the bats would stick right to your neck while you slept if you didn't drape mosquito nets. He and his friends would use rackets and swing at the fast-moving bats like swinging into the stars.

.........

Kris zipped the back of my Tyvek coverall after I zipped his. It was like wearing a giant trash bag with plastic footies and a shower cap hood. Last, we fastened on half-face respirators and safety goggles. The summer heat turned our coveralls into sweaty sauna-suits. But we did look official. Our task was to vacuum any loose debris that had collected in the attic. It seemed easy enough, but there were also years of bat guano to work through, which was why we were wearing the protective gear—guano, in excess and mixed with urine, is poisonous.

To remove the debris, Kris trudged a sixteen-gallon Shop-Vac through the crawl space to where I waited in the attic, standing on plywood between two beams, and then handed the vacuum up for me to grab by the handles. There were holes in the attic roof and floor, some small, some big, and light fluttered in while the guano fell out. Jana was on a platform lift, and I could hear her voice. While we were in the attic, Jana and Susan worked at removing and replacing drop-ceiling tiling in the church's main room. She told us to start where her flashlight was pointing. So, I stretched the extension cord and carefully carried it over, afraid to drop it, afraid to fall myself. It was not only difficult because it was awkward and heavy but because my goggles fogged when breathing. Whenever I tried to clean them, they smudged more. But what was really most challenging were the bats above my head that moved from one end of the attic to the other—individually or in swarms, like little grains or big black blankets, maybe a hundred bats but maybe more.

Kris joined me. He carried a box of industrial trash liners for the debris that was too large to fit through the Shop-Vac's hose. I kneeled, sucking up the unbound papers, loose splinters, nails, and God really knows what else. The vacuum hummed and coughed. I tossed an occasional item to Kris—*another Bible, one baby shoe, a tiny vodka bottle. Dude, found a necklace.* And to make ourselves feel better, we pretended we were treasure hunters. The vacuum, a metal detector, and Kris's hands were sifters. Kris would inspect whatever I sent his way. It helped us ignore any real danger, like being poisoned, being attacked by a bat, or simply falling through the attic.

.........

When my parents asked me about work, I was short on details. I knew what Mom would say. She would continue about how unsafe the job was. She would say how what we were doing was probably against some labor law. And I told her I was making more money than I was actually earning. Even though Kris and I received a raise, we were only being paid six dollars and fifty cents an hour. But Jana and Susan reminded us that it was tax-free money, so it was more than what we thought we'd make bagging groceries. We were also totally unqualified to do anything besides shovel horseshit or bat shit, for that matter. So, I told Mom I was making eight dollars an hour, and it mostly kept her quiet. But I did want to quit the job. Every day I contemplated it. Still, I couldn't because I was trying to prove something. I wanted to show Mom and Dad I was independent, that I could find a job, get the job, and keep the job. And even convince Dad that I was resourceful and skilled, as manly as any man with a hammer and nail.

.........

We filled the crawl space with half the box of trash bags, about fifteen that were one handful of shards away from bursting. We unloaded the bags from out of the crawl space, down the stairs, through the pews leading to the main room, past the altar, and then to the back parking lot. On our way, nothing looked like a church anymore. The carpet was torn and covered in dust and grime, and empty coffee cups, cigarette butts, and the fuzz of the old drop-ceiling tiles piled like snow. It was a complete renovation, and the projected completion time was a month. Jana and Susan continued working on whatever they were working on while we half carried, half dragged the trash bags to the dumpster, where we swung those trash bags as if some kind of Olympic shot put athletes, aiming into the dumpster after a three-sixty twirl. With each hit, dust and who knows what else billowed. *Nice.* I gave Kris a score of ten.

After we removed all the debris, we had to remove the guano. That was supposed to be the hard part. Back in the attic, we inspected the damage, panning our heads with the LED headbands, spotlighting corner to corner. What we had thought was relatively clear then became immense and horrific—for the sheer amount of guano was entirely visible, the mass of the thing: years of bat droppings and urine in the one closed space—literally, piled high, over a foot deep and more—and what seemed endless, was endless steaming piles of shit.

.........

Between filling my gas tank and buying lunch, I saved about four hundred dollars. It was the most money I'd ever had. I thought about all the things I could buy—maybe something for my car, a new muffler or subwoofers, maybe new sneakers and new clothes, maybe CDs and DVDs. Whatever I'd buy, at least I wouldn't have to ask Mom. Typically, I pestered her about buying anything. I didn't have an allowance, but she put money in my bank account when she thought I needed it. It was an account we shared. I had a debit card that I could only use when asking her. One time, I overdrew my account, and she nearly lost her mind. She took my debit card afterward and gave me a checkbook.

Being paid in cash meant none of that interaction would ever happen. But it wasn't just about the money, it was me being independent. Thus why I couldn't quit. Really, I hated the job, everything about it: the drive to Trenton, when all the gear in the van crashed from side to side; the church itself, that should had been condemned and torn to the ground; the smell, the taste, the moisture, the entire existence of the attic, like the purgatorial space between heaven and hell; and the bats, the damn bats that were always inches away from knocking me out. But quitting meant back to babysitting for free.

.........

We were shoveling the masses of guano that were more like giant termite mounds. We had to use little hand shovels because if we used normal-sized shovels, we could rip through the insulation. One of us held a trash bag open while the other dumped, and then switch and repeat. It felt like forever, taking a day to cover a couple yards—the attic, endless square footage. And the dumpster was becoming a trash heap, just bag piled on bag. We were supposed to wear respirators while throwing out the trash, but we didn't, at least until the smell became unbearable, like rigor mortis unbearable. And when the sun filled the entire sky, the bags melted and morphed.

We didn't see much of Jana and Susan. Susan ran errands back and forth to Home Depot. Jana moved up and down on the platform lift, rolled new carpet, discussed the progress with the pastor. The main room was looking better. The carpet was no longer a scab brown, but it was replaced with a soft strawberry red. The pews were refurbished with a strong-scented wood finisher. And though large sections of the ceiling were empty, the new tiles were stacked and waiting to be installed. Kris and I just had to replace the insulation since we were finally done with the bat guano.

We were an assembly line, passing the rolls out of the van, through the doors, into the church, up the crawl space, and there they sat until all the rolls were unloaded. They were large, about half the size of our bodies, but also light and easy to carry. We all wore gloves. Otherwise, the fiberglass in the insulation would absorb into our skin, our eyes, and our lungs, Susan said, so we also had to wear our Tyvek suits and respirators at all times. But the heat in the attic was unforgiving. And to get a moment of fresh air, we regularly pulled up our sleeves or took off our goggles and removed our respirators.

We thought installing the new insulation would be easy. It wasn't, not at all. Insulation ran between the beams on the floor and between the beams on the wall. First, we had to remove the old insulation that used to be pink but was now brown. When detaching it, turned-out nails and splints kept catching the sides, and we struggled to extract the insulation. Some were in full pieces, though most were ripped into segments, and it took about five or more minutes to remove each one. Once out, we bagged the insulation and threw the bags down to the crawl space and continued to the next section. We spent hours up there. Each roll was like ripping a giant scab off the attic—like the attic was this living, breathing, hot and hellish orifice, and every time a section was completed, the attic winced a little.

.........

The burning was unrelenting. My skin was so itchy, and not like an itch from a bug bite, but something different, something under my skin, parasitic. The fiberglass Susan warned us about invaded our eyes, our skin, and our lungs. We coughed constantly. But when Jana and Susan were nearby, we quieted, held it in, and let our eyes burn. It was the same when I went home. I tried to bypass my parents, with my eyes red and puffy, and my skin blotchy and irritated. Dad pressed me: *Are you guys wearing protective gear? You know that fiberglass can really make you sick.* Mom agreed and said that she better not find out we were not covering our skin. She threatened that she'd make me quit the job and take my car keys, and I'd be home for the rest of the summer. Part of me really wished she would.

.........

Jana said that we had to relocate the bats, reminding us that the name of the company was Extermination INC.—Pest Control, Renovations, and *Relocation*, and Management of Pesticides. *You can't just kill bats, that's illegal.* Now, very obviously, there would be no bat gun-traps. *To get rid of the bats, we have to get them while they're feeding. We have to find their exit point, wait till they leave, and then close whatever hole.* We were all outside the church, standing adjacent to one of its two roofs. One roof was smaller than the other, and Jana used a laser-pointer to direct our attention to where the second roof began. The red dot hovered. *Right there.*

Susan set up halogen tripods around the building while we waited for the bats to leave. The sun hadn't completely broken; it was that slow turning orange that would soon bleed red. It buoyed between the edge of the sky. Jana and Kris set up a ladder alongside the edge of the smaller roof. It slid around before steadying. *One of you will go on the roof and locate the hole and seal it with this caulk gun,* Jana said. Susan looked at Kris and me, and then Jana told us to stand back to back. We did. I tried to slouch. Jana said: *Stand straight.* I straightened. Jana handed me the gun.

Susan demonstrated how to use the caulk gun by pointing and pulling the trigger. I practiced without the caulk tube in. We still had to wait for it to grow dark. And when it did, minutes later, little shadows started flying out of the room. What first were a couple bats, became many more, in big dark patterns. The halogen lamps spotlighted their exit as they washed out the sky.

When all the bats were gone, Susan gave me the caulk tube. Kris held the ladder while I slowly pedaled up, keeping my eyes on each step, anxious in the way I'd feel before getting on a rollercoaster. At the time, I wasn't sure which I was more afraid of: falling from the roof or the bats returning or a combination of both. But I continued, one hand on the caulk gun, and the other on each passing rung.

When at the top of the ladder, about twenty feet higher, I looked down to Kris—*you got this, dude*. I pulled my body up and stood on the roof. The shingles moved under my feet. Maybe the entire foundation shook and everything that was keeping the wretched place together was moments away from falling apart, like *this is it*, the church would say, and then give up.

Jana signaled with the laser-pointer where I was supposed to caulk. It was literally right below the base of the steeple. When I was on the ground, that point didn't look so far. But now that I was on the roof, I realized just how far the little hole was from where I was standing. Jana signaled again. *Right there*, she called out. To reach it, I would have to stand where the smaller roof's sides met, where it became like a triangle.

I thought that all sixty-eight inches and one hundred and twenty-five pounds of me should not stand on a triangle; it was just poor physics. She signaled again. Reluctantly, I put one hand on the siding of the second roof to try and get my balance. I wobbled a bit. To reach the hole, I stood on my tippy-toes and—with the caulk gun in my other hand—aimed the nozzle in the direction of the hole. I reached, and reached taller, and pulled the trigger.

The caulk missed the hole and splattered white paste everywhere else. *Davon, look at the pointer.* Jana and the pointer were both irritated. I tried again and missed. Caulk everywhere. *Dude, it's right there*, Kris joined. I looked down, he was pointing with his hand, like that would do some good. I tried again, but before squeezing the trigger, I really stood as tall as I could, and pulled. The caulk seemed to purposely avoid the hole. Jana, Susan, and Kris continued yelling; I tried ignoring them.

*I'm coming down.* Completely defeated, I quit because I was damn near crying from fear, so afraid I would fall, and just too embarrassed to confront them, and embarrassed to go home and tell my parents, and even embarrassed to ever see a bat again. When I got back on the ground, Kris was holding a rope. Jana said: *Put this around your waist and Kris will hold you, in case you fall.* Kris nodded, and tightened his grip, *I got you,* and he bent his legs. *Go ahead,* Jana said. Susan handed me another tube of caulk.

# AFTER-SCHOOL
# BASKETBALL GAME

.........

SOMEWHERE near the Mason-Dixon Line, close to nothing much—a Wawa, Johnny's Farm, Smith's General Store, Carranza Memorial, and the high school where I sat in the gymnasium as red as a peregrine's eggs—where I stood between cross hairs, hothouse tongues, diesel and carousel, and steam, and where their heads were ready to blow, like 20-gauge loaded barrels. But also, in that gymnasium, one of the two of us could jump, definitely higher than the other, maybe higher than the backboard. And that one, when he grabbed the rim, he could hang there until the crowd roared. And that was the varsity starter—*look at him go.* His arms, almost elastic, stretching from one side of the court to the other, sending assists from under the legs and behind the back. *Give him the ball. I bet he'll make it. He can run. Boy, look at him run after that ball. Steal that ball. Shoot.* I was the other one, the one not playing basketball. And they watched me like a watchful mob—the heavy-duty Carhartt jackets, canvas dungarees, thick-treaded high-ankle boots, uniformed and still at war, camouflaged out in the open, eyes like deep mudded burials, eyes bone-white, sedimentary eyes, eyes full of such hate and history. And under those fluorescents, a basketball thuds, sneakers squeak, tracks around the three-point line, cheers, and then the silence of the buzzer-beater, like the silence when cement sets, like how muscles tighten, like how both of our Black bodies were sweating.

# THE BEST DANCER

.........

In the early 2000s, there were no how-to videos, no YouTube. I found *Breakin'*, the 1984 film, in my parents' tape collection in the basement. I'd toggle the buttons on the VCR, taking me to my favorite scenes—the rattle of bass and drumbeats crackling from the mono speaker, the cuts and scratches of the turntable, the claps of the crowd, the DJ's lyrics and ad libs, and then the bodies in motion, how they spun and flipped, how their joints popped and locked, how they synced to the music as if existing in rhythm. It was fascinating.

In my suburban town, their idea of dancing was do-si-dos, promenades, and allemande lefts. In gym class, we line-danced to "Cotton Eye Joe." Everyone counted the steps and sang along with the lyrics: fifteen four-person groups belting the chorus, wondering about Cotton-Eye Joe's origins and whereabouts. And then there was me, the Black kid, like a lone peppercorn in a salt grinder.

When it was my turn, I changed the dance steps—turned them into a grapevine, a take-it-back-now, a one-two-three-hop-this-time, a stomp or slide—and they watched, clapped me on, shouted my name. Instead of feeling alone, I turned the spotlight on myself as if to say *I will beat you to it*. But to breakdance, in comparison, was freedom; it was without order, fluid motion, stops and simultaneous starts, contortion, risk, a body upside down, balancing on one limb, a body in revolution.

Every day after school, I returned to my favorite scenes in *Breakin'* and for hours rewound, played, stopped, and learned. On top of a flattened cardboard box, I practiced the break-moves I saw. While other kids in high school played sports and participated in clubs, I was enveloped in that VHS time capsule, and that was as close as I'd ever get to a culture that did not exist where I lived.

I was cool if I could fit popular tropes, like the athletes in my town who ran fast, slam-dunked, and scored touchdowns. If you could be categorized, stereotyped, people felt safe. I decided that hip-hop and breakdancing was the part of Black culture I'd celebrate. I wanted to learn it all, from breakbeats from a boombox and Kangol hats and Adidas. I wanted to absorb it, to become it. But in this rural town, down these streets, sometimes paved and sometimes dirt, were lifted trucks barreling by with loud exhaust pipes, Confederate flags, banjo-and-beer blues, flannel, and hunting camo—everything that felt un-Black.

At fourteen, my identity and image were a collage of a single Black narrative. I wore FUBU, Timberland boots, and baggy pants. My hair was in cornrows. My Walkman CD player housed mixes of my favorite rappers. At school and in the hallways, someone would say *Davon, do that thing*, and the halls would split, all eyes on me, a chorus of *go, go, go*. I was compelled to do whatever they asked; I had become The Black Kid Who Danced. I would perform whatever new break-move I'd learned—my body flipping, fluorescents blurring, faces looking down at me, pointing, laughing, amused. I was a spectacle.

My peers wanted to play a role in my Blackness. Like when I'd wrap a kid's head in a do-rag, lapping the strings around the back, the front, and then tying a knot. He'd smile, showing the glint of his braces, and say: *Yo, that's dope*. He'd become a character in my performance, and I felt obligated to let him play, as if giving him a ticket to a minstrel show. He'd then contort his fingers into shapes and wave the *yo, yo, yo, gangsta!* He'd attempt an excessively intricate handshake, and I'd engage, white and brown hands clasped. He'd think I was cool, think I was like whatever Black character he knew from television. But in reality, I was more like him, more like those white kids, flattening what it means to perform Blackness, to be Black.

I won the superlative *Best Dancer* in high school. It was me against one of the three Black guys in my graduating class. Our classmates pitted us against each other and talked it up for weeks. It wasn't just about who was the better dancer, but who the cooler and Blacker Black guy was.

I was in direct competition with AJ, who was from Nigeria and would quickly say his nickname before teachers could mispronounce his full name. We were both afraid to be our true selves. AJ wore Abercrombie & Fitch, and I wore ROCAWEAR. AJ sang country songs, and I recited raps. We both assimilated under this white gaze, were expected to behave stereotypically Black, but also to be like everyone else, everyone white. Still, we had an understanding of each other, between classes giving a glance or a nod, something that said *we're in this together.*

For prom, we were to battle, like our classmates wanted; even the teachers took stakes on who was the better dancer. On the dimly lit dance floor, the DJ playing some version of *Now That's What I Call Music!*, the bulwark of bodies, suits and dresses pushing us in, demanded us to perform. AJ started with a one-two-step, lean-wit'-it-rock-wit'-it, Harlem-shake, and dirt-off-your-shoulder and finished with a side-foot-slide into a James Brownesque split. Everyone cheered and cameras flashed. Then he crossed his arms to say *you're next.*

I took off my black suit jacket and threw it to someone in the crowd, then told my buddy to hold my foot and push on three. We counted loud enough for everyone to hear, and he pushed me as hard as he could. I backflipped. For those seconds, I soared, and I felt good, like my Blackness was finally confirmed—that without a reasonable doubt, I was the Blacker of us two. I landed smoothly and hopped into a handstand freeze with one hand pointed at AJ, down to a six-step, and, finally, as if hitting a crescendo, to a head spin, and my black tie took on the motion.

Chanting my name, the crowd declared me the victor. AJ and I met in the middle of the circle to dap up and embrace. But really, AJ was the Best Dancer. He lost because he looked *too* Black, and I was *just* Black enough. I practiced those moves for weeks leading up to the prom. I'd even rehearsed the backflip outside my house with the kid who catapulted me. Nothing about it was freestyled, but it gave the impression of improvisation, which in many ways was like me—an impression of something else.

Though we never talked about it, to me, AJ moved through white spaces with such grace and cultural dexterity, knowing when to be himself and when to assimilate. I had no balance between being Black and acting Black. The two were inseparable. I was just a replica of the things I saw on television. But looking back now, AJ and I couldn't have existed without wearing the masks we wore. They wouldn't have accepted us any other way.

# THE BLACK JEW

.........

WHILE we stoically stood eyeing the underbelly of the Holocaust, in the Washington, DC, museum dedicated to it, staring at the pit of shoes that were gutted and spilled out—all the shoes in all the piles, the ones that didn't fit, the ones that were too large, too small, or didn't have the same size, those relics—all the feet, those ghosts, still somewhere in the soles. I tried counting just to confirm the horror, knowing I would never reach more than four thousand. There was no word or phrase or idiom in any language to express that ineffable history, what it meant to erase people—leaving only their rags, their bowls, their brushes, their spoons, their bones—their bodies summarized on the captions.

The air was sticky and cold. A disinfectant seemed to be pumping from the vents and left a slick resin on every surface. In long lines through each exhibit, slow and silent, as if at a procession for six million people, there was only the insistent *oh my God*, and then the realization of what little of God was actually there, or anywhere, for that matter.

How could we all not think of what we had—comparing life and death, health and illness, nourished and starved—what was in our pantries, our trash cans, our closets, however many coats, pants, socks, shirts, everything we had. How could we not shame ourselves then, disgusted by our material waste, disgusted by each breath we took and took for granted. How could we not think *what if there was something we could have done*, though it was decades before we were born.

Almost subconsciously, we had to consider, at least for a moment, what we would have done if on the outside. What if one of us was on the other side of the camp fence? What if any one of us could have slipped a wrist through the mesh, or thrown a bundle over the barbed wire? What if we could have offered whatever we had, anything, everything—and then what would it have looked like to peer deep into a pair of those eyes, as if gazing into the night and watching all the stars empty?

.........

We were escorted into a seminar room for a presentation. Rumor was, there would be two real Holocaust survivors. We rumbled down the lane, whispering and anticipating what we might see. When sat, we waited anxiously, not knowing what to expect, thinking it won't be anything like reading *Anne Frank: The Diary of a Young Girl* or watching *Schindler's List*. And at the same time, none of us really knew anything about Judaic history other than what we learned in school. In our small town in New Jersey, the Jewish population was almost nonexistent. We always had school on Rosh Hashana and Yom Kippur, and there were no synagogues, or Judeo-sensitive phrasing like Winter Break instead of Christmas. Rather, in our town, Judaism meant all those stereotypical things: collecting pennies, long pointed noses, yarmulkes, -bergs, -steins, -witzes, and kikes.

The two presenters, both women, were escorted in by a man who looped their arms around his. He looked as if he were carrying something breakable, as if counting his steps, watching the presenters eye the floor intently to avoid tripping. The presenters looked sort of indistinguishable from each other—old white women with willowy hair and skin that was almost transparent. Their bones gently shook. They might have been the same age, but maybe not. The women wore long cloaking dresses that draped over their skinny bodies as a coat does when thrown over a coatrack. They were so delicate, like two tiny twin birds about to nest. When they finally rested on the fold-out chairs in front of the audience, they sat erect, both positioned tautly. They leaned in, pulling forward, pulling us forward, as if to tell us a secret for the first time.

The man who escorted the Holocaust survivors was a museum representative. He sat next to them and his job, as he said, was to fill in any gaps in their narrative. He was a Jewish historian. If there were any questions, we could ask him after the presentation. Before the women began, he gave us a summary—about their concentration camps, their families, and showed photos of other prisoners on a projection screen. When he finished, he asked if any of us were Jewish or had Jewish relatives. No hands went up first, and then one, then two, then three. I looked around at about forty other students, only three hands up.

.........

I was always embarrassed to admit I was half Jewish, which sounds terrible, like admitting to having some disease. It was bad enough I was one of the only Black kids in our school, but to reveal being half Jewish meant I was going to be the Black Jew—a heritage of two of the most historically discriminated against people in the world. The litany of ridicule would never end. So, I never owned or affiliated myself with them. I never read the *Torah* or had a bar mitzvah or circled Jewish in any categorical box. If I were to identify with anyone, I considered myself Black because I was raised by a Black family and that's what my birth certificate said. So much of ethnicity is tied to culture, to upbringing. Therefore, I didn't consider Judaism part of my ethnicity, of my story, for the fact that I did not grow up with my father or my father's family.

Maybe I would have raised my hand if things were different, if I'd been raised by my father, a Jew. Maybe I could have embraced my other side, my other narrative. But as a child, I only knew part of the story, the part my mother told me—the part she knew. She had to tell me about my grandparents rather than me learning about them myself, from them. I had one picture of my grandparents, and it wasn't placed on my nightstand next to the picture of my mother's mother. This didn't belong there. It was hidden in a plastic baggie with some Polaroids of my father and me in a drawer I rarely opened. In the photo was my grandfather, grandmother, and a great-aunt. I sometimes would look at it, at them, wondering how those people were related to me. They were strangers, just people on the street. And yet, the blood that ran through them, ran through me. We were family. We had the same last name. But then again, we weren't family. Not at all.

My grandfather died when I was ten. I remember when my father phoned and told my mother. She gently called me into her room, sat me down and said that my grandfather had died of a heart attack. I remember wanting to be upset, wanting to cry, like how people do when losing a loved one. If it were my mother's mother who had passed, I'd know that emotion. I would have mourned wholeheartedly. I loved her. But not my father's father. How could I love him? The word grandfather, his first name, or even *stranger* were all synonymous. Yet still, when my mother pulled me onto her lap, I cried hard because I had to.

                              .........

The two women on the stage reminded me of my grandmother—not in an actual sense, but something about them prompted the thought. At the time, my grandmother was the oldest person I knew—eighty-nine years old. And she had that same fragility about her, like the stem of a leaf. And the same white skin that was like looking into a cell. And the mass of sunspots, and blue stringy veins—and that she too was Jewish. However, in no way were their lives and my grandmother's life comparable, and in no way am I trivializing the women's stories, and it's not my tragedy to exploit—their stories are not mine to tell. Though I can say, their presentation was unlike anything I or my classmates had ever experienced. It was as if being thrown into someone else's memory, a projection of a dream, taking on its sadness, its loss, its kind of death. They talked of when they were children—before, during, and after the Holocaust. And the feeling we all felt, like a contagion, our minds trying to understand something incomprehensible. Then again, maybe that's just human nature, to try to understand, to relate, to not only sympathize but empathize. We could never actually identify with those women and their stories, though, none of us could. What I did do however, I did imagine my grandmother. And I thought *what stories of her life could she tell?*

I met my grandmother about four times. After my grandfather passed, my father thought it would be a good idea for me to meet her, which seemed more like my mother's idea than his. Nonetheless, he and I drove to Long Island, New York, on a few occasions to visit her. I remember looking at her strangely, trying to find myself. She didn't appear much different from the picture I had of her, just older. I scanned her eyes, her lips, her skin, looking for anything I could attach myself to. She fed me a bowl of matzo ball soup and watched me eat it. She showed me pictures of my father when he was younger, pictures of her and my grandfather too. She walked me around her home and pointed to paintings on the wall. *These*, she said, *I painted.* From an old creaky drawer in a large dresser, she clasped an old newspaper scrap. It was a story about her and her paintings that had won an award. She told me this proudly. I remember feeling foreign in her little world, but also like I finally found a missing piece of something.

.........

I do think we were all changed by what the two women said, even if I can't recall the specifics without filling in whatever gaps of their narratives with what I've learned from studying the Holocaust in the years since. As if this veil was removed and the truth of the thing—of the Holocaust and its people—was exposed in the flesh, not a rendering of the story. This was something different, something tangible—an enlightened wretchedness, a visceral feeling in our guts and skin. After the presentation, students were invited to greet the women. A lot of us did, though unsure of what to say, but reaching out and touching their hands was enough, and it was terrifying, touching history like that.

The Jewish historian invited those who had Jewish relatives to search the Holocaust Survivor and Victim Database. On some level, I was excited to search my name as if looking for validation, for approval, for acceptance in this place, as if to say *I am family to this too*. On the kiosk screen, I typed my name, Loeb, and was flooded with the results. Just endless tapping of the down arrow. I didn't know what—or who—I was searching for exactly. Maybe some version of my grandmother, maybe a version of my father, or the version of me—one that would have been lighter, with curlier hair, a more hooked nose, some stereotypical Jewish characteristics I thought maybe I had. But the results were too many, just an indecipherable number of names, of bodies, of families. Maybe any of them could have been my lost relative or maybe none of them.

The Jewish historian said that if our Jewish relatives came from Europe there was a greater chance of one or more of them were Holocaust victims or survivors. And not that I felt honored to say *me too*, but I felt like something inside of me was here, and I wanted an answer. So, I thought I should call my grandmother, my father's mother. Maybe she could pinpoint my search—give me a name, a birthdate, a birthplace, something. I didn't remember the last time we spoke. And in a way, she was just as much of a stranger as the two presenters were. But what if? What if she had been waiting all this time to tell me about our family tree—about my lineage, about my Jewish history, maybe the origins of my last name, anything she knew. Whatever questions I was prepared to ask, I thought it would change something. I wanted it to change something. I wanted to feel like an insider rather than always standing on the outside looking in.

Outside of the museum with one hand on my ear to cover the back-to-normal conversations of my classmates, I called her on my cell phone. I waited and waited, listening to the phone trill anticipatorily. And then she answered. *Hi, Grandma. It's me, Davon.*

*Who?* she said.

*Davon, Harry's other son.*

# SOMETHING ABOUT LOVE

.........

IN the laundry room, after ignoring my father's phone call, after he canceled another weekend visitation, I stood with Mom hanging my head and wearing disappointment like a wet towel. Handing her a T-shirt, hesitantly, knowing she was going to feed me an excuse about my father canceling. *Why doesn't my father love me?* I asked. Her hand motioned for another shirt. She folded, sleeve, sleeve, length, collar, an assembly line. I offered another shirt. She focused her eyes on it. *Your father never learned to love.* And I thought how love was not a learned behavior, through conditioning and experience. Love was something instinctual, an undeniable trust and comfort in knowing undoubtedly that you are safe and wanted and accepted, an irrefutable thing, like the sun coming out tomorrow, and there's nothing more or less you can do on any given day to be unconditionally loved. But not my father—no. He was as indifferent as a shadow. Although unlike a shadow, he was there sometimes but more often not.

I asked Mom: *Did he love you?* And she waited a while

and looked somewhere else to remember, and her eyes held their blink a little longer. *Yes, your father loved me, but that was different.* Some clothes rumbled in the dryer. I wondered if that was how Mom felt, in that moment— like that dryer, her heart tumbling with memory-soaked emotions, and maybe her belly was spinning with recollections of my father on high heat. On the dryer lid, the pile of shirts stacked into a tiny tower that smelled like clean cotton. *He's not like us*, she said heavily as if the revelation to me saddened her. I anticipated what she would tell me next and pressed her with a sigh and an eyeroll. Maybe this time I would understand my father more. Maybe she had been withholding information for years, until this day, and now the truth would be told, and I'd finally understand why the man didn't love me.

*There is a lot you don't know about your father.* And she was right, for what I knew was just a retelling of the man, just her finger pointing out who is who in some old photos, just the stories about him and his other family, a life without me, before I was his son. I used to think that maybe it was my fault he was divorced—my fault he was alone and broken and sometimes a man and sometimes just a drowning man being tossed by the waves of life. I used to think that my birth was what ruined him, and that's why he didn't love me. *What your father knows about love is what his father taught him, which was only violence.* My grandfather, *an alcoholic with a loaded fist*, beat my father while my father's mother, the stoic bystander, *let him beat her son*, and *what your father is or what your father isn't is not entirely his fault*. She shook her head—*do you understand?*

# VISITATIONS WITH MY FATHER

.........

BECAUSE my father had no internet yet, we sat at the table flipping through the yellow pages. It was a Saturday night and wherever we went would have to be open on a Sunday, and it needed to be an hour away, max. But everything was far away, even the nearest grocery store was a twenty-minute drive. My father's house sank deep into Mount Pocono, and the seclusion was absolute. Sometimes the sun couldn't even break through the thick foliage surrounding the house, as if earth became the house and the house became earth. From the road, I couldn't make out what was what. The lumber and the bark blended. The smoke from the chimney billowed into the clouds till they were one. Thus, living in *the Nowhere* made options minimal.

My father told me if I could find a tattoo parlor open on Sunday and at a reasonable distance, he'd take me. Eager and motivated, I called the list of aggressively named places: Hell's Artist, InkBitch, Blood Shop. He watched intently from a distance, his eyes soft, focused, and constant, listening to how I spoke on the phone: the inflection of my voice, if I was polite, if I got frustrated. He'd look at me like that often, just steady, trying to figure me out, though the man was never actually critical. And yet, I always put on my best, whether I wanted something or not, always conscious of his judgment, thinking he'd say *so, this is how your mother raised you.*

My mother hated tattoos. And not just the thought of her sixteen-year-old son getting tattooed but tattoos in general. She'd threaten me when I came home from school with BIC pen designs on my arms: Chinese symbols, tribal art, rap lyrics. She'd say that only thugs and criminals had tattoos. Since I was neither, she would never allow me to get a tattoo while living under her roof. I couldn't completely argue with that. At the time, my two heroes, Allen Iverson and Tupac, were covered in tattoos, and they'd both had run-ins with the law. Not that I saw myself as a thug or a criminal. But I idealized those men, and their tattoos weren't mere body art, rather, they were statements, declarations of faith, pride, and confidence—Iverson's "Only the Strong Survive" and Tupac's "Smile Now and Cry Later." Those quotes were words to live by, and how could my mother not see that?

Visiting my father in Pennsylvania gave me the opportunity to go around my mother's jurisdiction. In Pennsylvania, minors could get tattoos if a parent consented. If I could convince my father to sign, all would be well. So instead of battling with my mother like I normally would when going to visit my father—me complaining about losing an entire three-day weekend when I could have been with my friends, about how my father and I didn't do anything except go to the movies and talk about school, and how being with him was like being with a stranger—I easily agreed to spending the weekend together. I thought my father owed me permission for a tattoo, if nothing else.

There was an art to convincing my mother: she'd say yes, no, or the quintessential *I'll think about it*. Thinking about it really meant I'd have to nag the hell out of her until she said yes, like the time I wanted to pierce my ear, because my brother had earrings and my friends had earrings; and of course, my life depended on getting earrings. I'd only pester her when she was too busy to pay serious attention, hoping to receive a half answer and then use it against her later. I volunteered to take out the trash every week with no complaint for six months if she took me to Piercing Pagoda, and she said yes to something else as well while handing me the trash.

Once I had the vision of a tattoo in my head, I was driven by the thought, obsessed, imagining what everyone at school would say. I'd be the only kid in our sophomore class with a tattoo, and everyone would revel. I swore, at whatever the cost, I'd convince her. Before the trip to my father's, I tested the waters while she was on the phone, asking if my father took me to get a tattoo, would it be okay. She was in between reading the mail, preheating the oven, and telling her girlfriend about her day. However many arms she had, she didn't have enough ears. She pressed one hand to the phone's mouthpiece, gritted her teeth: *Davon, I am on the phone*. I didn't care if she was on the phone, or if she yelled, or grounded me for a month. I was the fly beguiled by the flytrap. *Mom, Mom, Mom, would it be okay?*

.........

I didn't think he'd say yes. Hell, I didn't know what my father really cared about—what he deemed as socially appropriate or not. My mother focused on appearances, how I carried myself, how people might look at me. She grounded me for sagging my pants. She grounded me for saying *my bad* too much. My mother would say: *It's important that people don't look at you like that. It's important that you carry yourself with class.* But of my father, I only knew he preferred Mozart to Beethoven, Egyptian cats to American, wild-caught salmon to farm-raised. I had no idea how he felt about tattoos. He was my once-every-other-month-or-more-weekend-visit parent. He never told me what to do or not to do. How could he? As if pet-sitting a puppy he only saw a handful of times a year, my father just let me run.

When he still lived in New Jersey, my mother would meet him at a halfway point on the New Jersey Parkway, an equal hour-and-fifteen-minute drive for them both. As a child, I loved my father. I remember jumping out of my seat, a madman, so excited, as if on another playdate with a new friend. On those visits, my father let me do things my mother never let me do, and that was often the best part. It wasn't that he was negligent, but he let me explore our little designated visitation world freely, like when we drove around empty parking lots with me on his lap steering and him working the gas and brake pedals. My little fingers barely gripped around the leather-covered wheel.

We frequented a nearby park, where I picked out the biggest and limberest tree, the one that was daunting, the behemoth that touched the sky. I'd stand in its shadow, completely vanished by its trunk, and behind me, my father with his hand cupping the crown of my head would say *what's the plan, son?* Though we never made one, and I'd plant my foot in his two palms, and he'd bump me up to the nearest branch, and then follow, soundlessly, as if father and son apes ascending into the canopy. At the top, we saw cars on the busy roadways. We saw birds in flocks, people running or walking in clusters. We could even spot my mother hiding in her car. When she'd notice we were missing from her view, she'd rush out looking for us. But then she'd find me waving, perched way up there in a tree. *Hi, Mom.* She'd run toward the tree, yelling at us both. *Come down before you fall.* We never fell.

Gradually, something happened. Not a specific moment or an exact day, and I don't think my father just forgot about me, but he began to routinely cancel, the day of or when we were on our way. The excitement quickly left my body when my mother gave me the bad news—her look in the rearview mirror like she thought it was her fault. I remember the excuses she offered me: he worked too late, he was too tired, he forgot. I remember the feeling when my blood cooled from crying, the way my eyes stung, how my chest drummed, and the disappointment that struck a deep pang in my heart. I remembered thinking as a child did, personally and emotionally: maybe he just didn't want to be my friend anymore, didn't want to play with me, would rather be with someone else. My mother would try to cheer me up. She'd take me to McDonald's where I ordered a Happy Meal and then played in the McDonald's play area. There, I jumped up two stairs at a time, reverse climbed the twirling slide, scaled the ladders until I reached the top and sat there thinking about him.

.........

Early that day, he wanted to take me to the creek near his house. He said the waters were shallow for a stretch of two or three miles and easily swimmable. He planned to swim while I kayaked. He was adamant about taking advantage of the warm spring day but not pushy. Outdoorsy nature activities were his thing, cutting wood, hiking, freshwater swimming, but for me, not so much. I'd rather play basketball or video games. And I could do neither while visiting him in Mount Pocono, so I rarely came. It was a long drive, and if I went, I stayed for the whole weekend. No teenager wanted to spend up to three days secluded from the world, from his friends and hobbies and all else. In the couple years since he moved to Pennsylvania, I had visited twice. As I got older, I had no time for him. My weekends were scheduled for all-nighters, basketball tournaments, sleepovers, Sweet Sixteens, not hanging out with my father and being bored and being annoyed. I had my own life.

Whenever he called to set up a visitation, I was always ready with an excuse—I was working on a school project, I was sick, or I wouldn't even answer the phone. For I'd convinced myself I was too busy, too tired, too interested in a life that didn't involve him. But really, I was still that eight-year-old kid crying for his father, still feeling rejected, like he didn't choose me. When I was younger and the visits initially stopped, we went almost two years without seeing each other with no real reason why. And two years was a long time in adolescence. One day I was a hopeful child, counting down the days and hours until we were climbing trees again, and the next, I was a teenager who bitterly couldn't forgive and forget. After that, I thought, it was my turn to stop visiting. It was my turn to make him feel alone, feel how I felt, like he didn't deserve my love.

But on this visit, I agreed to the creek, thinking it would heighten my chances of a yes for the tattoo. So, I softened the blow, to get him right where I wanted him—between the ears and in the heart—do the things he loved, a father-son bonding experience. And there we went, with our shadows under the sun, carrying the kayak, carrying the flippers, and carrying two different optimisms. In my head, I heard him say: *If you want to see something beautiful, just go outside*. And in the outdoors, we experienced what the seclusion had to offer: the whirls of wrestling water, the hoots of deeply hidden birds, the trees that stood high, together and endless, as if all connected under one roof, one land. While walking over rocks and through puddles and pushing back twigs and bushes, I closely followed, tethered to my father.

………

My mother said: *Yes, if your father will take you*. But what she really meant was *he will definitely not take you, but if I say yes, you will finally leave me alone so I can finish what I was doing.* When she said that, I knew all I had to do was convince him it was a good idea. So before getting to Pennsylvania, I did my research—strong persuasion needed practice, planning, and purpose. I had to have an answer for why I should get a tattoo and what would it mean to me. I couldn't just say because I wanted one, because I wanted to be the coolest kid in school, because I wanted to be like Iverson or Tupac. I needed a real reason—something philosophical, something representational, like how Iverson's Chinese character meant loyalty. I loved that a Chinese character meant something else. And not that I spoke a bit of Chinese or knew much about Chinese culture, but I still thought it might represent me somehow. I also liked how Tupac had a giant cross tattooed on his back that said *Exodus 1831*. Like Chinese, I didn't really know what the verse in Exodus meant, I just liked how it looked. But the Chinese character and the cross were both symbols, which was the point—symbolism. I needed a symbol that defined me.

I also needed a tattoo I could relatively hide. If I got tattooed in a visible spot, my mother would lose it—lose it more than she already would when she found out. I was also aware of the taboo of tattoos in later life, in the workforce. I would not be that kid with the *No Ragrets* tattoo spelled incorrectly on my forearm. Iverson's Chinese character was on the side of his neck, while Tupac's covered almost his entire back. If I could combine the two, Iverson's character and Tupac's tattoo placement, it might work. I decided on my shoulders, my back, and down my spine.

Since I thought Chinese read vertically, the characters would look best there. I also wanted the tattoo to peek out just a little from the back collar of my shirt—enough that people could see it, but not enough that I couldn't hide it. And when they'd see it, they'd think *damn, that kid is cool.*

.........

The creek water warmed in the spots where the sun shone on it. In the shade, it was chilly. Listening to the stream pass over rocks and flow somewhere else was like putting an ear to a conch shell. I considered my thoughts: How exactly would I ask him? But the nature was a vacuum, and it was almost impossible to really think of anything besides what we were experiencing. I barely paddled, only the gentle current carrying the kayak. My father swam in long patient strokes, as if floating. It was amazing watching him. I could swim, sure—in pools—but not like that, in open waters. We traveled slowly and passed a man in rubber fishing boots casting a line. We passed a family of deer. We passed hundreds of trees I couldn't name. We passed over shallow waters where the kayak skirted across bedrock. But my father and I never passed each other. He'd grab the kayak whenever I strayed.

*Dad, I've been thinking about getting a tattoo*, I started, waiting a moment before continuing. He didn't say anything. *Dad, I've been planning it for over a year*, which was a total exaggeration. *My idea is a compass rose and Chinese characters down my spine that mean Manifest My Destiny, like fate, Dad—like the North Star. Anywhere I go, fate will control my destiny—it will manifest my destiny. I'll never be lost.* I pointed to where I thought the North Star would be, right behind the big frothy clouds. My father treaded water and listened. *I know it's a huge decision, one that'll be with me for a lifetime. But Dad, I believe it, in fate. And I'll get it on my back, so I can hide it if I need to.* We buoyed there a bit, not looking at each other, just the sounds of the creek washing over. I told him: *My mom said it would be okay if you took me.* I waited and then watched him like how he would watch me.

......... 

After calling however many places, we decided on a shop in Scranton, Momma Mae's Ink. This shop, unlike most in the area, was open on Sunday. My father and I only had twenty-four hours before returning me to my mother, so time was precious—we had to move quickly, call, make the appointment, no regrets.

He was impressed by my perseverance. And though I had no idea how to get there, he gave me a map and told me to find our route. I did, sort of, unfolding the thing on the kitchen table, looking for the road we were on, what major roads connected. I looked for Scranton in big letters. I tried to pinpoint where the shop would be, even penciled a dot. With his arms crossed, he watched, smiling gently, his thick mustache moving like caterpillar.

The whole way there, I stirred in the passenger seat anxiously. Throughout the months I had spent planning, I hadn't really thought pragmatically—how long would it take, how much would it cost, would it hurt? All I considered was the result. I didn't like needles, and who actually likes needles? My father and I never discussed a price. I just assumed he'd pay. How expensive was it? I had no real money, maybe forty dollars in my wallet. Regarding my pain tolerance, I could easily pull scabs off, pop pimples, and play basketball with five jammed fingers. How bad could it be?

On the drive, I talked freely to pass the time. My father listened eagerly while checking his mirrors before changing lanes on Interstate 81. I told him about the Maori, the people of New Zealand, who I thought originated tattooing. I told him how they used the sharpened bones of animals and the blood of insects and how I read all about it in a book called *Maori Tattooing*. I did my research, and my father agreed. I told him that someone in the village would dip the bones in the blood and then chisel the designs into the skin. *It took weeks, maybe months.* He nodded his head.

*Are you sure?* My father read my body language, the panning of my head, the cracking of my knuckles. He stopped the car on the quiet road that was leading us to the shop. We were adjacent to a small trailer park community. We had been looking for a main street, something with shops, but the address took us here.

I was scared, thinking about what my mother said. When discussing tattoos, she told me that people contracted hepatitis from dirty needles. She'd say: *How would you know if that needle is clean?* She was right. How would I? But the lure was too powerful. I thought the likelihood that this parlor would be the one with a diseased needle was rather slim, and what teenager doesn't think that way—that *this would never happen to me*, that *I'm invincible*. Not that I assumed I was actually invincible; I just trusted my father.

We would have to lie to my mom, at least, about where we went for the tattoo. I thought of every assumption about trailer parks, and the people who lived in trailer parks, and about sterility, about the needles being clean or dirty. And once the idea entered my head, the entire surrounding was tainted—the muddied street, the way the clouds sank low on the square rooftops like a fog, the way the whole damn thing took on some kind of loss—the cocked mailboxes, the broken-up fences, the cars parked without driveways, just stationed on dirt. And yet, there we were, slowly moving to the front of the trailer with the small neon sign that blinked: "Momma Mae's Ink."

.........

Momma Mae ran the parlor in a back room of her trailer. It was clean, as far as I could tell. It had the appearance of a white dental office and even that same antiseptic smell, like rubbing alcohol. She was eager and had greeted us eagerly after we knocked. She thanked us for our patronage. We told her how no other parlors were open in the area on Sunday. She laughed. *Momma Mae's open.* She was a very small lady, mid thirties, stout, and looked maybe like a Pacific Islander. Or maybe I just thought she was somehow related to the Maori. Maybe she was Maori. So, I told her about what I'd learned.

I'd brought a printout of the Chinese symbols from home. Prior to coming to Pennsylvania, I checked out a book from the library, *An Encyclopedia of Translation*,

to help me try and convert the English to Chinese. I hoped
the translation was right, but what did I really know?
Maybe Iverson's tattoo didn't mean Loyalty. Maybe all of
those tattoo catalogues in tattoo parlors—the ones in lan-
guages other than English, for people who only understood
English, people like me—were all being misled. Or maybe
not, maybe I was spot-on. So why not take the plunge?
Who did I know who could actually read it and say I was
wrong? Momma Mae appeared convinced, and so did my
father. Maybe it was fate.

I described a compass rose that she freehanded on paper
a couple minutes afterward. She showed me, and I agreed it
was right. She scanned the compass and the Chinese from
the encyclopedia printouts into stencil copies to stick to my
skin. When I removed my shirt, I was thankful the room
was cold—the air conditioner on full blast, cooling my
sweat. She placed one symbol down each knob of my spine,
and the compass rose pressed on my shoulders. She sucked
her teeth. *That's going to hurt, honey.* She jabbed my back
with a thick finger. *You got no fat there.* She pinched. *All
skin and bones.* I didn't care how much it would hurt; I accepted it. It would be my declaration—of pride, of faith, of
definition.

Momma Mae smiled heartily, like the lunch lady serving
the Friday pizza special. *No turning back, sweetie.* Before
applying the stencils, she shaved the little hairs on my back.
I jumped, startled, in anticipation. *You're okay, honey.* Her
voice was soothing, warm milk soothing. Then she stuck
the stencils to my skin like peel-off stickers. I sat on an in-
clined bench, facing a mirror, where I could see her work.

It was raining outside, and I watched the rain and listened to it.

My father said nothing. Part of me wanted him to, maybe to stop me, to tell me this was a bad idea. I smiled at him with a shaky lip. He had already signed the paperwork, on the dotted line labeled "Parent Consent," something he had never done. He had never provided parental consent for me before. Was he worried what my mother would say? Was he nervous if the tattoo would turn out okay, if it would hurt too much, if I could take the pain, if I would regret it, if he would?

.........

It's hard to describe the initial sensation when the needle struck, but it's the sound I remember most—the unstopping mechanical hum and the reverberations of drilling, the rattling of my spinal bones, like how cement sounds when hammered. I didn't say anything—I couldn't. My jaw was clenched so tight, the little masseter muscles locked. I gripped the bench cushion, showing the white of my knuckles. And in between hot-pressed grimaces, I could see Momma Mae work, her focus strong and concentrated, the tattoo iron inscribing like a chisel. And with every dab into the ink and each puncture of the needle, the stencils slowly filled.

I thought I'd numb after an hour—get used to the pain, suck it up, grit my teeth until they chipped. I said some mantra. I imagined all my friends in awe when I'd take my shirt off before jumping in the pool, or the girl behind my seat in class, telling her girlfriend that she could see what must be a tattoo peeking from my shirt collar. I even thought about my mother liking it, somehow proud of my determination. And all the while, I looked to my father unlike I ever had. I needed him in that moment, not just for the consent or the money, but for something else, something intrinsic. And I thought *is this what dependency feels like?* I wasn't sure, and I still don't know, nor do I think I ever will—or ever feel like that again. In those moments, if nothing else, I think that maybe my father was just showing me that he loved me.

# FOR MY BROTHER

.........

I had one photo of you. You stood by a small body of water, shirtless, holding a long wooden handle downward. I would imagine what you were doing when the photo snapped, give it a story—raking leaves on a warm autumn day, digging a hole for a pot of flowers, maybe a game of roller hockey. Whatever you were doing, you looked fascinating and perfect. You reminded me of one of those guys I saw on television—the Sitcom Studs with impeccably styled hair, imperviously fitted jeans, smiles as wide as bridges and teeth as white as cotton. Like some extra from *Saved by the Bell*, even your hair looked as flawless, as if gravity sliced it down the middle, with waves becoming curls, curls contouring clouds, like your hair was one beautiful Van Gogh painting. Your olive skin was soaked and saturated in the sun, with fiery tan lines around the forearms. I'd hold the photo like you were a celebrity and proudly think *how could you be my brother?*

.........

The first time I met you, we sat at my mother's kitchen table. Our father was talking to her, and you were chatting with me, completely engaged and interested. You weren't made anxious by the occasion—for the rarity of the thing, uniting with a long-lost relative, your brother. And though you earned the right not to be there, considering the situation—your mother was our father's wife at the same time my mother was his girlfriend some ten years ago, when you were around my current age. You judged not. You put whatever resentment aside and took the chance to meet your only little brother. I was overwhelmed with the newness. I paraded around all week, at home and school, telling everyone that I, Davon Loeb, have a big brother I've never met, and he's coming to see me. And there you were, an enigma, sitting across from me.

You asked about my hobbies, what I did for fun, a list of my favorite things. You barely voiced a word, just listened about my action figures, comic books, about which X-Men were the best, about McDonald's Happy Meals, and about the *Goosebumps* books I loved. I said how much I liked drawing, that it was my favorite thing to do. I'd prepared my sketchbook in case you asked, on the kitchen table. The papers were filled with turtles with muscles and swords. You asked to see, and I handed it over like a jewel.

I stood somewhat over your shoulder while you flipped through. *That's Leonardo*, you said, you knew from the blue bandana. *He's a Ninja Turtle, right?* I nodded like when someone asked if I wanted ice cream. You skimmed through more pages, and my eyes bounced between the pages and your face. *Hmm, good shading. Freehanded?*

*Impressive*. Your compliments were treasures. And then you asked for a pencil. I nearly ran out of my socks to get one. You drew a human figure: head, neck, torso, arms, and legs in seconds. Amazed at the accuracy and efficiency, I knew then that I wanted to be just like you.

.........

Hunched, you pinched a wad of tobacco from a Ziploc baggie and scattered it on a sheet of rolling paper. Methodically, you flattened the clumps, licked one side of the sheet, smoothed the paper, and then rolled it with thumbs and forefingers. A cigarette formed, and you perched it between your lips. You looked at me, while I curiously watched, and asked if I smoked. I was eleven then, and we were at our grandmother's house in Long Island. Surprised and a bit wide-eyed, I shook my head no. You lit the cigarette in the living room, but our father told you to go outside and smoke. And then, with heavy feet, you walked outside and slammed the screen door shut.

From a window, I could see the shoulder and arm of your thick wool cardigan flex and extend. You disappeared and reappeared between the building billows of smoke and the chilly breath of winter. I thought of the things I learned in health class about tobacco. I wanted to tell you about them—how your lungs would blacken, how you might need a voice box, how your teeth could rot—but your demeanor frightened me too much to say anything. You'd barely spoken a word to me or anyone since we arrived. Our father had driven me, and you met us here. You reminded me nothing of the young man I sat with over a year ago, when I was ten years old. He was charming, a listener, eager to converse, but you were cold, indifferent, and preoccupied. That cigarette burned slowly, for you lingered outside that window awhile. And when our father and grandmother talked to me about school and what I was studying, I didn't listen because I was focused on you.

When you returned, our grandmother sat us all at a little kitchen table with four bowls of matzo ball soup. You inhaled deeply, enjoying the steam on your face, and then warmed your hands near the base of the bowl. And suddenly, a switch flicked, and you talk vehemently, chattered about college, what classes you enjoyed, which you didn't. As if your spoon was a microphone, you demanded our attention—raving about what books you read in English and the theories you learned from Plato and some manifestos by Thomas Hart Benton and how statistics was a waste and what was the point of gen eds. I had no idea who those people were or the books you spouted, but like that matzo ball, I soaked up everything you said.

.........

My mother and I waited in her car at the usual drop-off at the McDonald's on the New Jersey Turnpike for my monthly visitation with our father. When the sedan pulled into the parking lot, with you sitting on the passenger side beside our father, I nearly jumped out of my seat in surprise. Our father greeted me with a hug. He tapped my head, *you're getting big*, which I was, measuring now above our father's stomach. I hopped in his car before saying good-bye to my mother. She reached through the open door to hug me, and she shaped her hand into a phone and mouthed *call me*. I scooted behind you to the rear passenger seat. You nodded and said *what's up*, as if I were one of your friends. I said *what's up* back and was amazed at how cool I thought you looked wearing a short beard, messy curly hair, and dark sunglasses.

We planned for a quick lunch at a local diner, but before going there, you said you needed to stop at an A.C. Moore art supply store. You were fresh out of canvases. I was thrilled because I had never gone to an art store, especially with someone like you, a real artist. My mother would tell me how you loved painting and drawing, just like me. And though I had none of your actual artwork, I still prized the sketch you drew in my sketchbook when we first met. You were an expert, I thought. I was merely an amateur and got my art supplies from Walmart or CVS, not an actual art store.

We had never gone anywhere in public together before, the three of us, so I wondered what people thought, if we looked alike. I wanted to look alike, and I watched your strut, and tried to strut the like you, slumping my shoulders and dragging my feet. You wore sandals, baggy light blue jeans, and a brown hooded sweatshirt. Maybe my mother would buy me the same clothes.

Entering the large warehouse, I wanted to ask you a thousand questions—what's that, what does that do, what's that for? But I held quiet, in awe of the seemingly endless amount of supplies. Determined and focused, you strolled to exactly what you needed, and our father and I followed a few steps behind. Of course, I also wanted to buy something, but my mother had only given me a fifty dollar bill for emergencies. I could ask our father—maybe I should have—but he only bought me something once a year, on my birthday. So I trotted silently, imagining what I would buy if I could: those charcoal pencils or that watercolor set and the ultra-fine point markers.

We stopped in the aisle where hundreds of different-sized canvases stocked the shelves. Standing behind you, I watched you measure the canvases by creating ninety-degree angles with your hands. Stepping back a little and then walking forward a bit, you looked through the hand-shaped box. You choose three of the same, about the size of a textbook. *Good*, you said. As we walked to the checkout, my head still swiveled rapidly, mesmerized by everything, and I decided a purpose for every package of pencils and paints and pens—what I would draw, what I would color, what I could create. But when we arrived at the checkout, I stood picking some lint out my pocket. Maybe you two forgot I was there for a moment and talked around me—about drying spray, oil paints, and your mother. On a rack near the checkout conveyor belt, I flicked at a pack of sixty-four Crayola markers. And as the cashier scanned your purchases and before our father gave you his credit card, you snagged the pack of those markers. *These too*, you said.

. . . . . . . . .

I was reluctant to stay overnight at our father's house in Teaneck, New Jersey, being that long without my mother, sleeping at a different house, a different bed, two hours from home, but you were visiting from college, and I wanted to see you. My mother even thought it'd be a good experience, maybe something she and our father would arrange more often. For how could I really know you or him when each visit was once a month for only a few hours? Instead, this was real together-time—wake up, eat breakfast, Saturday morning cartoons, more like a family. So I agreed and crammed a book bag with my most important things: a sketchpad, pencils, a set of colored pencils, two Spider-Man action figures, and a pair of jeans and T-shirts. Thankfully, my mother remembered, in Ziploc baggies, to pack my pajamas, underwear, and my toothbrush. She was nervous, organizing and reorganizing my stuff.

On the way to the drop-off, my mother reminded me again to call her when we got there, and after dinner, and before bed, and then in the morning. Impatiently I agreed. *Yes, Mom. Yes, Mom. I promise to call.* I wore bravery but shared the same nervousness. This was still relatively new. Our father and I had only begun to meet over the last five years. He was almost as much a stranger as you were. But still, I greeted it with excitement, wondering what we would do—maybe draw something, build a giant fort, play a board game, have a movie marathon.

I was in our father's room reading a *Goosebumps* book, and I heard you talking in the shower. At first, normally, as if a conversation between two people. When you spoke, you waited for a response. But there was silence, just the running of water, and then you spoke again. Only a room away, your voice was loud enough for me to hear the fluctuation in tone, from intense to friendly, a pattern developed. I tried to focus on what I was reading, but you grew angry, as if you heard something you didn't like. And then you screamed so loud and guttural, like the water was too hot or like your skin was burning—like you were hurt—and I nearly tossed my book. I heard nothing for a minute. My eyes were wide in confusion. You screamed again, louder, and it felt like the walls shook. *Dad*, I yelled, hoping he'd rush upstairs in seconds. Panicking and bounding off the bed into the corner of the room, I thought *where is Dad? Is he outside? How can he not hear you?* And then you continued, swearing and raving, arguing by yourself to yourself. A downstairs door opened and closed. Footsteps quickly traveled up the stairs while your voice reverberated throughout the house. You were a man in pain.

With the two of you in the bathroom, there was just screaming, voices climbing over each other. I couldn't make out who was who. And then threats and a scuffle. I was more frightened than ever and ran for the cordless phone on the dresser, scurrying back to the corner to call my mother. Hysterically, I told her to come pick me up. *Mom, please. They're fighting. Mom, Mom*, I begged her. She could hear them, and in her own dramatics asked: *What's happening, Davon? Tell me what's happening? Where is your dad? Put him on the phone.* I didn't answer her. *Mom*, I yelled, *please come get me now.*

My mother hadn't driven back home yet. She'd stopped to visit her sister, who only lived a couple exits down the Turnpike from my father. She got there in thirty minutes.

I never went back to our father's house in Teaneck again.

.........

You were sick then, and I didn't understand. My mom, however, used it as a warning, a reminder for me not to use drugs, not to be like you. She said you had a mental illness—that mental illness was in my genetics, like blue eyes—that *you are predisposed to having this thing happen to you.* She said I was predisposed to addiction, that one smoke or one pill or whatever drug could trigger it, *like what happened to your brother.* She told me that when in college at NYU, you started using drugs, that it was just pot at first, and then you experimented with harder drugs like cocaine and LSD, that due to your drug use, something activated in your brain called schizophrenia. Then, I didn't know what schizophrenia was. I asked her if you were crazy. She said you weren't, but you were sick and would never be the same. You'd always be medicated. She explained that was why, when I visited you and our father at his house in Teaneck, you behaved the way you did: *He was having a schizophrenic breakdown.* She told me how our father experienced his own battle with addiction, with alcoholism. Just like our grandfather, she told me. *Honey, this is why you can't ever use drugs because, unlike some of your friends, it may affect you differently. You can become sick, like Alex.* My mother told me how people were all born with some predispositions to sickness and disease, and mental illness was just the same. I was so sad then, thinking about you as the young man from the photo—how then, you were everything I thought I wanted to be.

.........

I was seventeen and hadn't seen you in years, but I was still eager to be near you, like being near some tortured artist. You, our father, and I all met again at a diner in Hackensack. I sat next to our father and you were across from us. Our father and I discussed the usual—school, friends, my mother—carrying on, filling the two hours until my mother would come pick me up. You said nothing and just watched me while I chatted and stuffed down two Belgian waffles.

*How are you, Alex?* I had exhausted things to say to our father and directed the attention to you. You shuffled with a messenger bag next to you in the booth. You said you had a surprise for me and lifted a book from the bag and placed it facedown on the retro-style diner table. I reached to flip it over, but you said: *Wait, not yet.* So, I waited, anticipatorily, and spoke more about what movies I liked and what music I was listening to. You abruptly stood up and said *I'm going for a smoke.* Then you pressed your forefinger on the book and said *this is for you.* You asked our father for his car keys and walked out of the diner. I waited for the ring of the bell on the door to flip over the book you left for me, and when I did, it was a book of poems written by Alex Loeb, you, my brother.

You were a real writer, I thought, and sat amazed flipping from front to back cover—reading the "About the Author," your name, your face, your words. Published that year, in 2001, I read the synopsis out loud at the table with our father listening proudly: *This book of inspirational poetry lightens the spirit as it seeks to inform. The author believes that poetry is a path to enlightenment and comforts those who are seeking the truth.* My eyes rounded and hovered across the photo on the cover, a painting of clouds, mountains, and the moon. *Dad, Alex really wrote this?* Our father said you did. *Can I have it?* I tightened my grip on the slick and smooth paperback. *Yes, it's for you.* I opened it and saw you had signed it: *To my brother, Davon.*

I skimmed through the crisp pages of the book, quickly reading lines of the poems in my head. I wanted to talk to you about it—talk about what inspired you, if you got writer's block, how you published your book. But you never came back from the smoke. You sat in our father's sedan doing whatever it was that I couldn't see. So I continued to read until our father paid the check.

.........

The only poems I had read up to that point were the boring poems from school: "The Road Not Taken," "Fire and Ice," "We Real Cool." Those were not poems by someone I knew, by my very own brother. I read your book endlessly. I brought it to school, showed my friends. *Look, that's my brother.* I told my teachers and read your book during any free time. I memorized your words, like a song. I recited them, sometimes while riding my bike or doing my homework. I talked to my mother about it, every day almost. *Can I read you one?* And she'd listen to whichever poem. I imagined you writing your poems, somewhere under a tree

or at a coffee shop. I longed to talk to you about all of it—
*why did you use that metaphor* and *that simile? How did
you come up with that title? Teach me how to write like
you.* But I hadn't seen or talked to you since you gave me
your book at the diner.

*What do you want to be when you grow up?* As a child,
I wanted to be a painter like you, a painter or a cartoonist.
After your book, I wanted to write poetry, be an author,
write just like you, maybe even write my own book. So, I
began writing, taking parts of your poems, borrowing the
words, the sounds, the cadence—and collecting my poems
in a little book I promised would be published one day. I
wrote a poem about you, a response to your book:

"The Story of His Poetry, dedicated to Alex Loeb"

*The timeless wheel spins with the momentum from the
unchanging breaths of the morning sky. Early fall leaves
drop by and by. Collecting at the bottom of the tree
where the indomitable soul conceives perpetual art.
With an intention of exclusive fulfillment, he draws the
brim down because the wind propels in the course of
his face.*

*Rather cold but awakens what has been incarcerated
in his mind.*

*It has possibly lain dormant from the time of birth,
till now, or from yesterday, till tomorrow.*

*Hard to tell, but its undeveloped nature is what sets
it apart from any other thought. A moment of spiri-
tual revelation arises and what has been vesturing in his
heart, cries onto the canvas.*

*Enviably, we endure the same emotion he felt upon creation. And a fallen star falls, but yet, once it rose with the intention of success.*

*We feel its suffrage, and it gives us our own reasons to reach for the sky.*

.........

Later, I discovered our father had paid to self-publish your book, though that didn't make it lose its luster. I wanted him to publish my book of poems. I researched the cost—about a thousand dollars, including an editor, an evaluation, and an on-demand printing contract. Promotion was entirely the responsibility of the author. I could handle that. My collection was around a hundred pages, like yours. I divided it into three sections: about love, about life, about my future. I was seventeen then and full of dreams. My poem to you would be featured first, for you were my inspiration.

I wrote my own proposal and sent it to our father. I waited a week before calling him to ask about it. My voice trembled in anticipation and excitement. *Dad, did you get my letter, the proposal?* He said he received it. *Well, I was hoping you could pay for me to publish my book of poems. I wrote one Dad, like Alex.* Before he could really respond, I said: *It's really good, Dad, probably as good as Alex's. I can read you one.* He paused on the other end, then *I can't afford it right now. I'm sorry.*

And I kept thinking: *You did it for Alex, paid for his book. What about me, why not me, aren't I your son too?*

But I didn't say that. I just accepted his response. After that, we didn't talk for a while, not for six months, when he came to my high school graduation.

.........

I was visiting our father for the weekend at his apartment. He was swimming in the first-floor swimming pool, but I had declined the invitation to join him and was reading some book for school. His cell phone rang four times and when the fifth call came in, I thought it was important and answered. On the other end, you hung with a voice that was broken, and you said: *Hey, Dad. Dad, you there?* I responded that it wasn't our father but was me. You stuttered some, like trying to pull your memory together to identify who you were talking to, like you were trying to recall my voice, and maybe you did know it was me but maybe you didn't. You said *oh, tell Harry my grandmother died*. I responded that I'd tell him. You ended the call, and I tossed the phone back where I found it.

*Your grandmother*, I thought. You called to tell our father that *your* grandmother died—not *our* grandmother but *your* grandmother. And then I thought, *you're right, she really was never mine.*

Our grandmother died at ninety-eight, and I didn't even know she was in the hospital. I didn't even know she was sick. I had spent the entire morning with our father before he went swimming, and he had told me nothing. I wish he had. I wish we had all waited together in our grandmother's hospital room, anticipating her passing, watching her chest heave and fall, listening to her heart lose its beat on the monitor. We'd be together, like a family, recalling moments of her life, our memories with her—like when she forced me to eat matzo ball soup and olives, when she showed me her paintings in her house and in that Long Island newspaper, when she said I looked just like our father, how you and I looked so much like brothers. Those were the only memories I had of our grandmother, and I hadn't visited with her in years before she died. So instead of a grieving father and his sons gathered around his mother, their grandmother, I was alone in a studio apartment thinking of what it might have felt like to actually mourn, to experience sadness and loss, to feel like I was as much her grandson as I was your little brother.

.........

The last time I saw you, I came to visit you and our father for lunch near his new home in Mount Pocono, Pennsylvania. I can't remember any of the other diners' names our father and I had gone to over however many years, but I do remember this one, Twin Rocks Diner. I was in college, studying English and education, still writing, I said, presenting a neat summary of my life. Our father had retired from dentistry. You, as I learned, were living on Cape Cod. You looked so very different from how I remembered. The Alex I knew was thin, the body of a swimmer, and handsome: defined cheekbones, thick curly hair, a scruffy beard. But the man sitting across from me was someone else entirely. Your full head of curls now receded, and the once slim frame had thickened—your body appeared swollen, in all parts, even your face was puffy—and your eyes were sunken, like a man holding his breath. You were almost unrecognizable.

At lunch, I listened more than I talked. I knew who I was, my everydayness, the man I had become, my past, my future. I wanted to hear about you—my estranged brother. And though you looked like a different man, I was still captivated by you, like I was as a child when we ate matzo ball soup at our grandmother's table, how passionate you were then about everything you said, as if your next thought were always some new uncharted territory. And now when I asked you what was new, you told me with that same bravado. You talked about returning to college, taking classes at the community school nearby, and you might start painting again, maybe sell some of your work—for thousands you were sure—and your next poetry book was about true enlightenment, being close to the stars and to Zion, and sometimes you went fishing off the coast of Cape Cod, and one time you caught a fish and brought it home and skinned it and cooked it, and you reminded yourself of a man named Santiago, and you were going to lose the weight, after you changed your dosage, you just had to figure it out, probably in a week or so, or when you got back up North, and you had an interview for a job that you knew you'd get, never mind what it was, and you were happy to see me, and you said just how much I reminded you of yourself. And while your mind was a pinwheel of fantastical ideas and plans, I knew none of it was really true. I wanted it to be true, part of me needed it to be true. Some sort of a happy ending.

.........

My mother always told me you were so much like me, *kindred souls*, she said. And though you and I never grew up together, somehow, she was absolutely right. All the characteristics that make me who I am, to the very core of my heart—my desires and aspirations to be a writer, an artist, a dreamer, what has filled my days since I was a child—is of that same stuff that coursed through your veins—creativity, imagination, ingenuity, and sensitivity. My mother would say I didn't get it from her side of the family. *Isn't it funny how genetics work?* Everything I am is everything you were. And regardless if all the stories my mother told me about you were true, it was beautiful mythmaking. She gave me a piece of my family that I would never have.

I have loved a stranger ever since I was a boy. While these feelings I have for you are real and certain, I haven't seen you in years. I think you still live on Cape Cod, in a residential facility for adults with mental illnesses. But maybe you don't. Sometimes you phone me, and I ignore the call. Sometimes you leave a voice message, and I don't listen before I delete it. I never visit our father when you're there, and I'm not sure why. Maybe it's safer because you're sick, so I can keep my distance. Maybe if I pretend you aren't here, you won't be. Maybe you'll forget about me, and maybe I'd prefer it. Maybe I'd feel safe, away from you. And maybe I'm just afraid to become you. I am afraid that something will trigger in me, as it did in you, and that something will cause my life, like yours, to loosen—to scramble, like a mind that has found itself lost in itself— that this structure I have built, my life, will crumble—that something is wrong with me too. Denying you is denying that—denying that we are really brothers.

# LIVING IN A STUDIO APARTMENT

.........

WE were strangers there in the dark, me listening to my music to drown out your snoring, while living like cellmates in your studio apartment. Mom thought it'd be a great idea—save money, get to know each other, spend quality time. After all, it was the first experience together for more than a weekend, just the two of us. The apartment in Hackensack, New Jersey, was on the tenth floor and was finished with hardwood, granite countertops, stainless steel appliances, the upgrades, and even a swimming pool, fitness center, door attendant, and balcony with views of New York City. And it was free.

You agreed to let me stay. I couldn't say no because Mom wouldn't let me. No matter how much I refused, she said *either live there or do another year at community college.* She said maybe I should have studied harder in high school. *Why didn't you earn a scholarship? Your future is in your hands*. So what if all my friends were away and living at school. *You have to do what's best for you.*

In the dark, palming the back of my head, like you used to do to me on visitations, staring into the ceiling, I imagined dorm rooms with posters of John Belushi. I imagined the coffee shops, sitting with other students on laptops studying through all-nighters. I imagined the dining hall, an array of options—wok, grill, salad bar—perusing the sections, looking for friends and a place to sit. But instead of the quintessential college experience, I shared one thousand square feet with my father, me on the futon and Harry in his bed, less than a yard away and still further than two continents.

......

While I commuted to Montclair State University, you worked Monday through Wednesday in the Bronx; and after work on Wednesday, you drove and stayed at your soon-to-be retirement home in Mount Pocono. If my schedule was successfully planned, I could mostly avoid seeing you all week. Classes started at noon, and I drove two hours from Mom's house, where I stayed on the weekends, and then to campus, where I stayed for the whole day until nine, by which time you were in bed. And when I got home, if I could call it that, you were asleep. With eggshells under my feet, I showered, ate something from the microwave, and plugged into my music, my headphones rocking me drowsy as if a child seduced by a mobile—to the voice of Sade, to Dexter Gordon's saxophone, to the piano keys of

Thelonious Monk, to guitar chords of Jerry Garcia. And in the morning, me facing the wall, half squinting, half awake, I pretended to sleep until you were gone.

In those mornings when you trailed to-and-fro as if waltzing from each square inch to the other during your a.m. routine—brush teeth, shower, coffee, newspaper— you played your music on low. Soft classical songs ebbed from the six-piece entertainment set—crescendos, decrescendos, and the melodies you tapped out at the kitchen bistro table. I might have enjoyed those songs and that time together with you. I could have sat, drank coffee, talked of school, the girls I dated, what classes I studied, the music I loved. We could have shared something in that brief hour, maybe catch up on all those years we were just weekenders, just a forty-eight-hour-long father and son. But I was too angry, too glued to the past: the missed birthdays, basketball games, dinner dances.

For the rest of the week, I lived alone. Every Wednesday, just after you left, I swung open the blinds as if Moses splitting the seas, and the sun spilled out, and I celebrated, a twenty-one-year-old college student living alone in a studio apartment overlooking New York City. And though I longed for the college campus, I could settle for three days of this independence. I felt like an adult. I was an adult. I went grocery shopping. I cooked dinner. I watched the late-night movies. I left crumbs on the couch. I paraded in my underwear. I lived in your space and tried to make it my own—invited friends from school to my studio apartment, drank beers on the balcony, and gazed into the New York

City skyline as if staring into the stars and pinching them with our fingers. I was proud of this little space for the moments when we did not share it.

.........

Sometimes when you were gone, I'd go through your things thinking I'd get to know you more. It'd be easier than actually talking. Maybe I'd find a photo album with pictures of our family I had never seen, maybe a picture of you when you were my age. I wanted some mystery, some revelation about you. And if nothing, maybe I'd find a remnant of myself, a school picture, my adolescent basketball trading card, a letter you wrote to me that you never sent—something that bound us, besides our last name. But in your nightstand, only balled receipts and loose change. In the kitchen, just plastic flatware and chopsticks. In the closet, two coats and a pair of shoes, for it seemed you were a minimal man, with no sentimentality toward the past.

However, in the almost barren apartment that shone no windows into your life, your memory, or your heart, there was a sculpture on the dresser that puzzled me. There, exhibited, the body of a woman, nude from the head down to the navel. Cast of wood, she appeared captured in mid motion, her hips tilting to one side, her arms following her hips—all moving as if in a dance. I'd find myself staring at it, sometimes uneasily, as her wooden eyes fixed on me while I tried to sleep. And in a way, she was seductive, how her body gave itself to the unknown looker, how she welcomed the gaze with a face of contentment, with the posture of pleasure. It was an odd and an exciting feeling, watching her, waiting for her to move.

One morning during your routine, feeling spontaneous or just haunted by wonder, I turned out of my shell. In a rare exchange of dialogue while you drank your coffee before work, I asked you about the seductress. *Dad, where'd you get the sculpture from?* Surprised by my question, you stopped mid sip, uncrossed your legs, and walked over toward the sculpture. One hand holding your cup of coffee, you touched the bare shoulder of the wooden woman with the other. From the background, overtones of string instruments accompanied your movements, in sync and almost cinematically. I shuffled on the futon and dug out of my blanket, ready to listen. You brought a chair in from the bistro table. You placed it in front of me and sat, then smiled proudly, your lips curving in a way I rarely saw them, though reminiscent of how you smiled at me when I was a child.

You said *I made that*. Unprepared for that answer, I sort of sat there, arched my brows, and *humph* was all I could get out. *I molded it first by clay*, you said, *and then took it to be cast into wood. She*, you pointed, *was someone I loved.* You continued, eyes in a long blink: *Not your mother though. I bet that relieves you.* You laughed and so did I, understanding the joke together. *I did sculpt your mother once. It was my most beautiful piece.* And then you fixed on me, as if studying me somehow, somehow searching for something you might have lost. Your eyes glowed then, brighter than usual, like when fireflies first

light. I sat up. *Where is it now, the sculpture of my mom?*
That moment and question hung a bit, like the fumes of a
lit pipe and maybe you were thinking of what to say next.
I was waiting for it. You put your coffee on the floor, and
the steam that blew off reminded me of a Van Gogh painting. You leaned in, your elbows on your knees and your
hands at your chin: *Well, after things didn't work out with
me and your mother, I threw her,* he stopped to clarify, *the
sculpture, in the Hudson.*

# THE MAKINGS OF
# A GYM RAT

.........

I think it all started with cartoons. Saturday morning at ten, I sat cross-legged in front of the television. I was always on time for *X-Men: The Animated Series*. Mom would have pancakes or a bowl of cereal ready and a kiss in exchange for breakfast. I ate sitting on the living room floor with the food on a tray, humming the theme song with a full mouth. I don't know how I never missed my mouth because I never took my eyes from the screen, passing fork from plate or spoon from bowl mechanically. This was my Saturday routine, like how Dad would drink coffee and read the newspaper or how my mom phoned her sisters.

Those thirty minutes were precious, but the episodes ended so fast. Did the X-Men survive? Did they get Magneto? Is Wolverine really missing? Is Jean Grey dead? I tried to predict the next episode. I'd tell Mom, while handing her my dirty dishes, what had to happen next. *Wolverine had to be okay, right Mom?* I think she listened, or pretended to. And if she wasn't on the phone, I'd ask her: *What mutant powers would you want?* This was important. Maybe the most important question in my life. *Would you want to control the weather, Mom, like Storm, or be like Rogue and absorb powers?* Mom typically picked Storm because she liked her white hair. And impatiently, I waited for her to ask me who I wanted to be like. It was a toss-up, but the power I wanted most was super strength.

At school, my friends and I discussed the mutants we most wanted to be like: Gambit, cool and suave; Beast, intelligent and kind; Cyclops, the bravest and most heroic. But Wolverine was our favorite, with his enhanced strength, agility, senses, superhuman healing, and an Adamantium skeleton with retractable claws. Wolverine was snarky, furious, unforgiving, valiant, and above all and in every facet of the word, strong. He could shred Sentinels as quickly as he could pierce through steel doors. I'd pretend, along with my friends, we were him, using his famous line: *I don't know what corner you crawled outa, Bub.* We ran around the playground using sticks for claws.

And it wasn't just their superpowers I wanted—I wanted to be built the same. All of the X-Men were strong, their muscles etched from deltoid to abdomen to quadriceps. Even the women had the same physiques: muscles on top of muscles in spandex uniforms. That's how we thought superheroes should look. Wolverine had abs like knuckles. His pecs were boulders. His biceps were rocks. I could wear the same yellow and brown mask, but I would never really look like him—not as skinny as I was.

.........

I had a toy chest of action figures, which included my favorite superheroes: Wolverine, Spider-Man, Cyclops, Gambit, Magneto, Iron Man, The Incredible Hulk. Every time my parents took me to the store, our local Walmart, I raved and begged to buy another figure. They avoided the toy section, but somehow, we'd end up there. I think I was addicted—collecting more characters, more bodies—addicted to the anticipation when reading the description on the back of the package or the satisfaction when ripping open the plastic covering. But I think I was more addicted to storytelling, to creating worlds and backstories and plots and actions.

This was a quintessential experience in becoming creative, of being someone else, making stories. When not watching the shows or reading my comics, I put on my own episodes, taking on the heroes' voices, their demeanors, their attitudes, their superpowers. Some girls played with dolls, played house, drove Barbie around in her Barbie car; I flew the X-Men on my model Blackbird in my bedroom.

The action figures were three-dimensional re-creations of the cartoon or the comic. It was as if the characters were really there with me, in my world. I'd face Spider-Man against the Incredible Hulk, yelling, *Hulk Smash! Bam! Ka-pow! Wumpth!* in my best onomatopoeic voice and throwing Spidey to the other side of the room. During an intermission, I'd run for a peanut butter sandwich snack with a big glass of milk. I'd sneak it into my bedroom and offer a bite to Hulk. We'd pretend, and then he'd say *drinking milk makes strong bones, makes Hulk strong. Be strong like Hulk.* So, I always drank my milk, hoping it would transform my spaghetti arms into the giant bulging biceps on the Incredible Hulk figurine. I often compared myself to these superheroes—feeling their plastic muscles with my fingers, tracing the striation, the definition—and then doing the same thing on my body—my concave chest, my ribs that I thought were obliques, my ruler-like clavicle, the way my legs were pencils and my arms were lead. And I'd look in the mirror, flexing, wishing I were one of them.

.........

After middle school soccer practice, I rushed home to watch *Dragon Ball Z*. Goku, Vegeta, Piccolo, Krillin, Yamcha, and Tien, I kept these characters in mind while running sprints and doing push-ups and sit-ups. It'd be worth it. Goku trained in his Gravity Machine up to a hundred times over the Earth's gravity. And although these were cartoons, I still admired the characters' perseverance— their resilience to be better, stronger, fitter. The story lines and plots focused on Goku, the hero, from an alien race of warriors called Saiyans. And after every battle, every close-to-defeat, Goku became more powerful. I considered that was, at minimum, worth watching. That at least I could adopt the mentality that hard work paid off. But really, I loved the show. I loved the characters—how their ass-kick-ings resulted in them eventually kicking more ass.

By this point, I was thirteen and too old for action fig-ures. But I had enough sketch paper to publish a textbook.

So, while watching *Dragon Ball Z* from my bed, with my graphite pencils and sketch pad, I routinely drew the characters: starting with their boxy heads, spiky hair, thick necks, shoulders that almost connected to their ears, triangular torsos with big chests and a small waist and an eight-pack, and then attaching the lower body, splitting the four leg muscles, shading the definitions between them, curving the calves by drawing semicircles. I could draw these people, either man or woman, in seconds, without looking, because they were running in my imagination like a filmstrip. And when finished, I taped my drawings to my bedroom walls, as a constant reminder of my goal.

.........

My older brother, Troy, like the many fictional men I idolized, was born of brawn and might. While the superhero characters were imaginative depictions of the ideal male's physique, my brother was the real thing—a body carved with God's chisel. I used to think that maybe my brother's very chromosomes were better than mine. Since we didn't share the same biological father, Troy seemed to be gifted with far superior DNA. As children, he ran faster and jumped higher than me. His body had the build of an athlete, his torso like an inverted triangle: broad shoulders and chest, a small waist, a wide back. Furthermore, everything athletic was easy for him; I swear I never saw anyone throw a football any farther. With perfect form—three fingers on the laces, thumb at the button, index finger at the tip, feet shoulder-width apart, ninety degrees at the elbow—like lighting the end of a cannon, he could throw that football across an entire street block. And at the receiving end, I'd wait nervously, my hands in front of my face in the shape of an oval, knowing I'd probably drop the ball.

Without even working out at the gym, Troy was naturally muscular—his workout was only push-ups and sit-ups. I'd watch him before bed and do the count. Like an untired robot, moving its gears and cogs, he mechanically pumped his piston like arms until reaching fifty push-ups. He'd say one hundred push-ups a day, fifty in the morning before school and fifty at night before bed. As if an instructional video titled "How to be a Man, How to Grow Strong, How to Get the Perfect Body," I listened, observed, and learned. Troy told me that when I could do fifty straight, we could work out together, just he and I. And I didn't know what was more motivating, the promise of hanging with my brother, or the potential to actually become as strong as him. On many nights when I knocked to enter his room, Troy and I counted to—and way beyond—one hundred.

.........

Initially, my push-up form was terrible—my elbows turned out, my butt in the air—barely doing a consecutive ten-rep. So, I modified for some weeks—resting on my knees and then doing the proper form. My arms trembled, like branches of a small tree in a windstorm. At any moment, I thought, my little humeri might snap from taking the weight of my body. But I kept at it, and no major changes at first; but after a month or so, I was stronger. I could do twenty reps consecutively. I'd rest, and do twenty more, and then ten, reaching fifty. In those mornings and nights, the floorboards creaked rhythmically like a snare drum.

This was high school, and everyone's bodies had started to change—some rounded, some thinned, and some became more muscular. You could tell which kids always went to the weight room: the football players and wrestlers. They were stocky, bulky, lean, cocky with reputation, like soldiers marching through the hallways. Their bodies had refined themselves—growing from the two-a-day practices and regimented daily consumption of a half dozen hard-boiled eggs. But my body stayed the same: a whopping five feet seven, hundred and twenty pounds, still fitting my youth-sized underwear and T-shirts. I never managed the courage to step into the weight room after school. I'd walk by the entrance and hear the weights bang and the boys slap hands, hoorays, and then those guttural grunts my action figures used to make.

.........

Mom always told me that God made me this way. And I was skinny because she was skinny and my father was skinny, and *honey, those are just your genetics.* But who wants to be told that? That your body is the body you will have forever because that's how genes work; that due to genetics, like having eyes the color brown, you will look exactly how you look because that is the way you were designed—that was God's plan.

I don't blame my mom because that's what moms are supposed to say. She would also tell me how kids used to make fun of her when she was younger because she was so skinny. And while her sisters had curves, the bodies of women, my mom had none—a body like a washboard. They called her Raggedy Ann. But now, my mom would say: *Look at me. I'm still skinny, but I'm married and happy.* I'd return with *and you're beautiful, Mom.*

This never really changed how I felt. There was a deep longing for something different, a different me. It became an obsession, more push-ups, more sit-ups, more filling a bottomless hole. Eventually, I convinced my parents to buy an old home gym machine. They searched yard sales and bought one for cheap. It included a lat pull-down, chest press, leg extensions, and cable-curl bar. This would change everything. I'd do real workouts with real weights. And those *Dragon Ball Z* photos I had drawn and posted on the wall were taken down and replaced by my favorite athletes, the men I idolized—the ones I wanted to look like, the ones I wanted to become: Arnold Schwarzenegger, Bruce Lee, Ronnie Coleman. And in the basement where the all-in-one equipment was, I went to work.

Sometimes Dad ventured into the adolescent-scented space, often to tell me to be quiet. I worked out late into the night, thinking the more I obsessed, the more progress I'd gain. And Dad, most likely following Mom's orders, told me to save it for another day—tomorrow I'd definitely be stronger. And though I knew the answer, I always asked Dad to exercise with me. While using whichever piece of equipment, I'd load the heaviest weight I could add. Using all my body weight in addition to some strength, I'd try to impress him. *Dad, look.* I jerked the EZ curl bar from my waist to my chest, exerting more lower back than bicep, while the veins in my neck bulged, and I grunted as if being punched in the belly. If I was lucky, Dad humored me and would say *Davon, I'll show you.* And then he would. Gripping the bar, he'd effortlessly curl whichever weight I'd used, doing at least twenty repetitions. And his biceps grew instantly, surging with blood, becoming the size of a fist-shaped rock. Dad, impressed with himself, would say *Davon, add more weight.*

.........

On many weekends, my best friend, Nicholas, slept over and lifted weights with me. He went to a nearby high school and was on the football team, so for him, working out was an everyday routine. Thus why I'd try to impress him, show him my max-weight of whatever exercise. And then, nonthreateningly, he'd say *let me try.* He did, but doubled my number, lifting the weight easily. Then I'd try that weight and almost burst a blood vessel, fighting the bar down, using all my body weight, jerking and shaking. Realizing my frustrations, Nicholas was never cruel or boastful about being so much stronger than me. Sometimes he used the same weight but pretended to struggle, to make me feel better.

I swear, even Nicholas's mom had muscles. I remember being at his house while she was curling dumbbells, hearing the bars ting and her grunts bark from their upstairs loft. I remember wanting her to be my mom. Maybe she'd give me better genetics. She'd birthed Nicholas, who was basically born with a six-pack and twelve-inch biceps. So maybe if my mom looked like her, I'd look like him. Even though I spent hours in that basement pushing those weights, like trying to push something out of me—with each exhalation, maybe I would change, something, anything—I still didn't change. Nothing. I hadn't gained a pound or become more defined or stronger. And in my frustration, watching Nicholas gain the body of a man, I grew jealous. How could I not compare myself to him?

Whenever we hung out with girls, they always liked Nicholas more. He looked like the guys on television, the heroes in movies, the centerfold in *GQ Magazine*. And yet, he never became conceited. He deflected compliments he received by telling silly jokes. And if any one of those girls wanted to feel his arm, he'd fart on her, and whichever girl would scream and scramble. As naive as he was to the girls' attention, he was always conscious of me, always—of my feelings, my insecurities. So, after the girls left, like a crowd of fans, I'd thank him. *For what, man*, and then he'd punch me in the arm. We were thick as blood; we were brothers.

Lifting weights was our thing, our bond. He took me to the YMCA and showed me how to bench press. It was my first time in a real gym. And having him with me, I was less anxious about what other people thought. So what if I dropped the bar on my chest, which happened during the first set, and almost crushed my sternum? And then the time I got stuck in a squat under the heavy barbell, a hundred thirty-five pounds, my legs seemingly ready to break like a turkey's wishbone. Or when doing a skull crusher, and I actually crushed my skull—the curl bar dropped on my forehead. It was all embarrassing, sure, but Nicholas helped me recover, every time, with no ridicule. *Try again, bro*, and I tried again, and again. And with each session, with each breakdown of my muscle, the fibers tearing and then repairing, I became stronger.

When we turned seventeen, I got my driver's license. Instead of paying for a gym membership at the YMCA, we drove to McGuire Air Force Base, where my mom worked. Children of military parents could go to the gym for free. So, there we were, two boys in a pit of men—real men, military men, who epitomized strength. It was intimidating in every way. Those soldiers, hardening their bodies, like sharpening a sword. And while Nicholas and I wore Converse sneakers, they wore combat boots; we wore basketball shorts, and they wore fatigue pants. For them, this was an everyday routine, like brushing teeth: wake up, eat, run, train, clean rifle, be strong, "Army Strong—Be All You Can Be." We idolized those men—mimicked their workouts, talked shop with them in the locker room, ordered the same protein shakes. And while they were preparing for some war, we trained for the attention of girls and fist bumps from our reveling peers.

.........

I'm surprised Nicholas and I didn't join the military. Maybe it would have been the perfect schedule: sleep, eat, work out, repeat. Simple, the three essentials. But instead, Nicholas and I attended the same college and remained tethered at the hip. And there, nothing changed; we still idolized those gym bodies—the ones we called Gym Rats. Those were the guys who spent every waking hour at the gym, whose uniform was a string-tank-top-tee and fitted gym shorts, who carried a gallon of water and brick-sized protein bars; guys who lived in the gym, there no matter what time we went, morning, afternoon, night—there, tan and lifting weights, breathing heavy. Crowds gathered around these young men, Nicholas and I included, worshipping their muscular improvements, their *gains*—like the guy with the huge quads the size of tree trunks, the one with the giant chest like two beer barrels, the dude with the sixteen-inch biceps.

Nicholas's ripped and well-defined frame took to the exercises well. All the workouts from high school influenced his body's ability to grow and maintain muscle easily. Not to mention, we ate an enormous amount of campus food—maybe thirty-five hundred calories a day. Half a dozen boiled eggs, two burgers with no buns, globs of tuna salad on rye. He gained almost fifteen pounds of muscle after starting college, and his strength improved tremendously. He went from bench pressing two twenty-five for three reps, getting to at least fifteen with no spotter. And the same crowds that gathered around those upperclassmen, whom we adored, started to circle around Nicholas. *Come on bro*, the crowd would cheer.

Eventually, I gained weight and muscle mass too, almost ten pounds. I started college weighing one thirty-five, and then, after a year, weighed about one forty-five. Finally, my body changed. My flat chest morphed into something more muscular, rounded, and I even had stretch marks running through my skin to show the growth. My pencil-thin thighs thickened, as if a sapling sprouting into a tree. My back widened, and the lateral dorsal muscle broadened like wings. And in a way, Nicholas and I turned into those same Gym Rats—our old shirts lost their sleeves, our language changed to speaking in roars and grunts rather than actual words; we evolved while devolving, like apes thumping our chests. I think I spent more time counting to ten in the gym than I spent studying in the library.

.........

After college, I became a certified personal trainer to make extra money. I thought it would legitimize my obsession of achieving some perfect body, a perfect me. Paying seven hundred dollars for books, online lectures, and examinations hardly made me an expert, but it gave me the certification required for the job. I was convinced that this would finally advance me to the next level of fitness. If I knew everything about exercising, I would have to exercise better, a foolproof plan. And when I got a job in the gym, maybe my clients would even want to look like me, their idol—for I spent the majority of my life trying to look and become like other people, from my cartoons and action figures to my brother and my dad, Nicholas, and those military and college men who epitomized real-life strength.

When I landed a job, I took pride in being a personal trainer. It was all I talked about to clients, to friends, to family. If a conversation about exercising or eating healthy started, sometimes without me remotely included, I chimed in *have you tried?* It validated me and my obsession, for I loved being the person who had an answer for weight loss, muscular pain management, and diet and nutrition. And while my hubris grew, I tried to remain humble, kind, and empathetic to my clients, considering the goals I'd had all my life and the advice I sought in those men I admired. On the exterior, my body changed, and from a perspective other than my own, maybe I'd achieved the ideal physique; but internally, the war raged—the insecurities raged like Jupiter's red storm. My calves were still too skinny, my abdominals were still underdeveloped, my V-shaped torso was more of a *U*. However much progress and improvements I made, my life still seemed minuscule, as if the clay were still oddly shaped, still unformed. And always during warm-ups before my boot-camp class started, I'd say *don't compare yourself to the person next to you, just be your best self, focus on your workout.*

.........

Even today when I judge myself, I see something that other people don't see: I see my dysmorphia, me trying to change my body's composition from muscle fiber to shirt size. I see an unfinished picture, one that keeps erasing and reetching, just bigger biceps here, thicker thighs there, a flatter stomach. I see a body that is not mine, as if a collage of *GQ Magazine, Muscle Magazine* cutouts, Instagram fitness influencers I follow—the idols I've worshipped and the parts of their bodies I've glued on, trying to achieve my masterpiece. And for however many hours—ten thousand or more—I've spent exercising, thinking about exercising, meal prepping; however many boiled eggs, grilled chicken breasts, and cups of brown rice; however much money

I've spent on supplements that promised the best results, to improve my strength—*this will change your life*—whey protein, weight gainers, creatine, pre-workouts, BCAAs, glutamine, testosterone boosters; however much I've done, I am still no closer than I was as a child watching *X-Men: The Animated Series*, or playing make-believe with my action figures, or obsessively drawing the bodies I wanted. I am no better, no different, because this hole in my identity is the bottom of a landfill, and the bigger I build, the deeper and mightier the underneath grows. No number of sets and repetitions will ever be enough. I am still empty, just an impression of some perfect and unreachable self, an unblemished apple on the surface but one that is rotten on the inside. I will never feel complete, whole or fit enough, big enough, strong enough. I am obsessive and compulsive and insecure. I don't exercise for the right reasons. I never skip a gym day; it comes first—before family, friends, and love. I am idolatrous, searching for false hope in the Gods of Perfect Bodies, the ones I've always wanted as my own, the bodies that I'll never have.

But then again, I keep telling myself *if I do just another rep.*

# IN-BETWEEN SIRENS

.........

THE in-betweens are like waiting for something to happen, like flashes of red and blue and sirens pulsing through my car. The in-betweens are when the police officer is about to step to the window when I am watching him from the rear-view mirror and unsure about what will happen next. The in-betweens are the statements my mother told me to say— to call him sir or her ma'am, to be polite, to be well-mannered. The in-betweens are the seconds it'll take me to open my glove compartment for my paperwork and then move my hands to the steering wheel, keeping my hands visible. The in-betweens are the moments after, the moments when my stomach is completely buoyant, and my eyes are blurry from tracking the officer and the patrol car's lights. The in-betweens are when his flashlight is sizzling on the back of my neck, *but I kept the speed limit, my seatbelt was fastened, I used my right blinker when pulling over, my vehicle is in good standing, I didn't drink or smoke weed and the friends in the back of my car didn't either, and we were just coming home from dinner and driving back to campus. And shut up, don't say nothing* is what I tell myself because the in-betweens are when the police officer knocks on my window with the back of his flashlight, but I am too afraid to look. The in-betweens are how long it takes for my window to lower and when he tells me to step outside the vehicle—to exit slow, to keep my hands where he can see them, to tell him my name and hand over my license. The in-betweens are my friends' thoughts, those Black and brown boys in the back seat whose faces are shined on by the other policer officer around the rear with his flashlight, the officer inspecting my car, targeting the light's beam on my friends, whom he has also instructed to lower their windows, asking their names, *Terrance*, but then the police officer says *Tyrone* and Terrance says *Terrance*, and then police officer pans to the face next to Terrance and asks the same question. The in-betweens are the steps I will take outside my vehicle, one foot over the other, and the time it takes for me to count backward, starting with seventy-two to one. The in-betweens are the breaks between each syllable in my name when the police officer reads my name back to me from my license, how he asks if I really am *D-A-V-O-N*, but he doesn't attempt to pronounce it right, and how he then checks my face against the face on the license with his flashlight that he hasn't let go of, and how I rest on the hood of my car and my heart rate is rising, and how I didn't do anything wrong, and I know it, but I tell myself to *shut the hell up*. The in-betweens are the things I don't say because I know exactly why he pulled me over, how he said there'd been a string of burglaries in the neighborhood where we were driving and we looked suspicious, and how I'm not a bit surprised.

# A SMALL LESSON
# ON LOITERING

.........

WHEN my mom tells me this, I'm seventeen and impatient and *yessing* her for the car keys. She does this often. Holds me here, hostage, in the kitchen, between the dinner table and door, but I'm just trying to hang out with my friends, and my eyes are aimed on those keys, and her eyes are watching me, staring as if afraid to let go. A fear cements her like she knows what I don't. *Mom*, an inquiry and an imperative, *it's just a couple friends, no drinking.* She wears worry in her eyes, and it's always there before I leave; it's deep and distant, like she's considering something she doesn't want to. She can't even sit there comfortably, uncrossing and recrossing her legs.

*What's wrong, Mom?* I don't think anything is actually wrong, but she wants to talk to me, so I sit, slouching like a scarecrow. The keys clank on the glass table. She says *you know it's different for you than your friends; you know that, right.* She slumps her shoulders to match mine. *Listen, honey. It's different for you*—I finish her statement: *Because I'm Black, right.* But not really, not like her. I'm just a brown kid with curly hair, and I confuse people. *What are you,* as often as a greeting. And my mom tells me what I am every day.

She's tired and her scrubs are wrinkled, but her hair is neat, the color of dark licorice, and she smells of perfume and antiseptics. This is how I recognize my mom—beautiful, and yet broken off and somewhere else. She reaches her hand out to touch mine: *Did you know your grandmother's uncle was handsome like you?* She dabs her finger in my chin dimple. *He was a little older, but was funny and cute with your grandmother, teased her and bought her things. But on a Saturday in Alabama when he was walking downtown and doing nothing much but chatting and gossiping like young kids do, a group of men, police officers*—she stops to find the story.

It's not that she's forgotten, but it hurts to tell it. I can see it in her face, how her brows shift, and her lips tighten. My mom is a strong woman, not physically, like muscle and brawn, but she's resilient—a poor Black girl from Newark who joined the military at nineteen and didn't come back home; she eventually became a nurse, and after years of service was a major in the Air Force. But this story shakes her. *He was so charismatic,* she chokes on the words, and when she's describing him, she looks like she's describing me. Our hands are back together, and she rubs her thumbs hard on my knuckles. She releases her clasp. *The police charged him with loitering because back then, if you were Black on a Saturday night and not home and were in the streets, you were breaking the law.*

My mom has been telling me these stories all my life— about my history, my family. Pass-me-downs, from her mom and her mom and her mom, and sometime before that, a language that wasn't ours. But these stories are how my family created people—how we buried them, how they were resurrected, how you could breathe life into someone just by remembering a name, making whole their body and then telling their story. She told me about my great-great-grandfather, a slave in Mississippi, and my one uncle who marched in Selma, and about the sit-ins and protests and all the things my people did for me. But my hands were typically in my pockets wrestling with lint.

It's summer now, and the cicadas and crickets are singing. There's a break in the blinds and the moon slides in. I'm sitting at the table with my mom, and my friends are waiting, and I'm wondering if it was a night like this, if my grandmother's uncle was just like me. So I imagine him: his black skin in a bright yellow open-collared shirt, showing his chest, and his pants might have been rolled up, his ankles bare in brown oxfords. I imagine him singing a song from the radio, and he sounds like Nat King Cole. His hair is parted, and he smells like sandalwood. He sees friends at their homes, on their porches, and calls out their names, smiles and strolls on. He can hear the cicadas and crickets too, but they sound different in Alabama. He's happy, and plans to join the army soon, just after he makes his girl his wife. And in between the chorus and verse, a police car spotlights him.

My mom is afraid as if she's always afraid of what hasn't happened. It's frustrating because I think I know everything. To me, these are just stories, things of the past. And I say *Mom, that was forever ago. It's different now. Mom, Mom, look at me. No one even thinks I'm Black.* She blows breath like smoke from her nose. We're both resting on our chairs, studying each other. *It doesn't matter. You're Black enough. And what about your friends. You think they'll get in trouble too; you think they'll have the same consequences?* This is because my friends are white. She pauses; the fan above the table is spinning. Even the insects outside break, and it's almost silent, just an electrical hum. And then she continues *your grandmother's uncle was killed that night, in his holding cell. They beat him to death.* She quickly covers her mouth, like she's snagged her tongue. And this time when I imagine him in that daffodil-colored shirt, it's bloodied with red dots and smears. His handsome face is bruised and broken and a black that is unrecognizable. His body is crumpled in the corner, and the suspended light bulb buzzes a bug and flickers, and those three men, whoever they were, are laughing in the distance.

My mom's fear has surfaced. She's the mother of a Black boy, and no matter how much lighter I am than her, I'm still Black and in danger. She believes it's not a matter of if, but when. She knows she can't protect me but hopes these stories will.

# ON THE CONFEDERATE FLAG

.........

I'M driving behind an old Ford pickup on State Highway 70, cutting through the New Jersey Pine Barrens. The road is straight and thin. No neighborhoods, gas stations, or stop-n-shops, just a distance between here and there. The travel is longer this way, but there's no traffic. In between mile markers are entrances to dirt roads, some large enough for a one-way vehicle and some only for an ATV. Yellow "Deer Xing" signs are frequent. And on either side of the shoulder is an endless growth of trees, an incomprehensible green and brown that can't be deciphered at this speed. The sun hasn't set yet and is still stretching itself on top of the tree line like a red and orange mist. It's easy to get lost here, to make one wrong turn—maybe end up between cross hairs or bear traps. The cell phone service is poor and so is the AM/FM.

At this point, I'm in silence, except for this truck that is motoring slowly, and its exhaust pipe chokes like the engine is cutting off. I'm in a rush but can't pass over the double-solids. Smoke billows, and the dual rear-wheel tires kick up dirt whenever it accelerates. The truck bed is rusted, exposing the primer. Still visible, though the paint is chipped, is the glorified red, white, and blue "Stars and Bars" Confederate flag on the tailgate. There's a bumper sticker underneath; I speed up to read it: "Heritage not Hate." I stay on the truck, pressing the gas, almost tapping the hitch—wanting to touch it. I recognize this rage. I've felt it before; it hollows me out, like being struck in the gut. But the air doesn't escape; it stagnates and buries deep inside of me. This rage, it fills my lungs, sharp angry breaths, the kind of fight-or-flight breathing. I want to fight. I want to hurt something.

.........

You and I spent so many nights like bugs, growing and changing rapidly while cocooned in our sleeping bags and staring at glow-in-the-dark star stickers on the ceiling. Eighteen years ago, we talked of what little life we had, which girls we liked, who would start in that weekend's basketball game. We shared the secrets of our families— the things our parents argued about, which siblings we loved more. It was as if we put an ear to each other's hearts and said *I'll listen to the things that make you happy, that make you sad; I'll care. I'll be your friend.* That's why it hurt so bad. It's always the ones closest to us that break us the most.

At first, the change started small. You traded your Sixers jerseys for hunting camo, the leaf-patterned shirts, hats, hoodies. It seemed you wanted to blend in, so we stopped playing basketball together, and then the sleepovers ended.

Instead, you followed those dirt roads into the Pine Barrens and found yourself different; you found yourself a better shot on a trigger than with a ball. I was as disappointed as any kid would be when losing a friend, as if something was cut off from me. But the real betrayal was one day in home-room, before the hallway chatter and bell-ringing commotion, when you sat far from me and pointed out—to some other kids—the front of your new shirt. They said things I don't remember but clapped their hands and rallied attention. And then, as if just to face me, you turned your torso. I saw it, the Confederate flag imprinted on your chest and in large letters, "Mississippi Justice," and what looked like a noose dangling from the center.

I wondered how you could just become someone else, how your body could remain the same but your heart could change, how this thing—this celebration, this honoring, this remembrance of bigotry—could bud inside of you and grow, grow quickly and easily and as encompassing as any teenage fad. And yet, you had eaten breakfast at my house, at my parents' table, with my Black parents. My friend who had watched every NBA Friday night tip-off on one of our couches, sharing a bowl of anything. Because everything in those moments mattered. My friend who had picked scabs with me, then smeared our blood, pressed our hands together, and swore we were brothers. When I saw that flag on your shirt, and the rope, and the allusion to lynching, a switch flipped, and I was on you. Ripping at your shirt, driving with hands—open, closed. Angry hands. I wanted to open you up and pull out the hate that I thought was inside. I wanted to find it and ask you why—why you hated me.

.........

My family originates from Mobile, Alabama. I spent summers with my cousins, happy in that heavy, humid air, slurping water from dirty hoses, magnifying ants, and chasing down the ice cream truck. On many nights after a plate of my grandmother's crispy chicken and mac 'n' cheese and collard greens, my cousins and I stumbled belly-out full onto her porch and sang with the choir of cicadas. We caught fireflies in mason jars, and they looked like stars. We drank pitchers of sweet tea until our teeth ached. We talked with a twang, as if trying on a new language. We were kids exploring the territories of summer life. We hung on to each and every moment, like holding a bead of sweat—the freedom of our bodies with no schoolwork or bedtimes, the joy of ripping off a shirt and feeling the cold spritz of water from the sprinkler on our backs, how we'd arch our spines in surprise and excitement. But we also learned the rules of living in the South while living as a Black child in America. We learned why we couldn't play outside after eight, when the sun sank and the streets emptied. We learned about the danger of skin, how the hooded boogeymen, as we called them, would come and get us. We learned about the fathers and uncles and brothers and boys who hung in that blanketed darkness, how they were ghosts, how they were strange fruit. We learned about three little Black girls at the 16th Street Baptist Church, about heaven and that's where they went. We learned of the word *impunity* and how it means you can get away with it. We learned that this, too, as Langston Hughes said, was America, and that there's blood here, in the Southern ground. It's inside those plantation properties—the shacks, the fields, the home. It's in the trees, and the willows weep because they remember it. It's in the foundation of communities, towns, cities, states—the statues, the names, the flags, the economy. The blood of slaves grew a nation. And this blood is inside of me. When I think of "Heritage Not Hate," when I think of the Confederate flag, when I think of a noose, all I can think of is a narrative, a cultural and ancestral narrative, that is of a time and a place and a people who were measured by their monetary value. But this isn't just a criticism of the South. I cannot paint a picture with one stroke. You can still love the South, your home, where your memories are full of laughter and family and beauty, like my memories; you can still honor a place whose history is rich and thick as honey. You can eat and dine and find comfort in its special palate; you can read its authors, its literary masterpieces; you can listen to its music—the soul, the blues, the rock; you can revel in its culture. But you cannot deny that its past is deep-rooted in the pain, suffering, and destruction of Black bodies.

.........

We all drove trucks in high school; it was a part of our community culture. Rangers, RAMS, Frontiers, Tacomas, Silverados—like choosing clothes, it's how we fit in. Mine was a '97 Ford F-150, blue, V8 Triton, Flowmaster exhaust tip. It rumbled, and so did the twelve-inch subwoofers in the cab. On any given Friday night in October, a parade of trucks pulled into the school parking lot. It sounded like a monster truck rally, engines revving, music volume maxed, and all the trucks would come sporting new gear: lift kits, double-tread tires, roll bars, mud flaps, back racks, pole mounts. *Truckin'*, they called it. Nothing different besides who our school football team was facing. The opponents one Friday night were far-out-of-towners who looked vastly different from the faces in the stands. Their bus pulled in slowly as if unsure they were at the right location. The football players in maroon uniforms stepped uneasily out the bus, guarding their equipment, panning left and right, anxious in a way that had nothing to do with the game. An off-key orchestra of banjos and guitar riffs and drum kicks and big voices was deafening. Kids sat in their truck beds on lawn chairs and sipped cold beer from red cups. They yelled things the players couldn't hear and felt good saying it. Mounted on one super-duty diesel waved a thirty-six-inch Confederate flag. I watched, from the seat of my F-150, the brown and black faces of those boys from the other team as they walked over the pavement and stared in disbelief, in fear, in anguish. I felt that way too; I was angry. I was always angry, and ashamed that I had gotten so used to it.

.........

On early Saturday autumn morning, when the air was crisp and cool, when the grass was slick, and the trees shook loose their stubborn leaves, whisking to the ground, my father and I tirelessly drove and dragged the tines of lawn rakes into what was left of the brush, the leaves, the pine needles, and the sweetgum pods. We created a collection of piled and pigmented foliage, browns, greens, reds, oranges, and yellows, and in between the sound of the rakes clawing at the dirt, warblers were warbling, sparrows were trilling, and a woodpecker was knocking into a spruce tree. These Saturdays, when the sun stretched carelessly across the billowing light blue, cloud-crowded sky, our neighbors in minivans would slow and honk their horn or wave from the windows and stop to ask how our day was going, and from those back seats, a friend from school would invite me for a sleepover. How little I thought—or we thought—about my skin or his skin. How little we knew or cared for what differences separated us. This place, the New Jersey Pine Barrens, where I rode my bike in the backyard wilderness, where I cannonballed into the soft surface of some great lake, where I was safe, is what I called my home. In this place, there are also twenty-one known hate groups, and these people were my neighbors.

# RETIREMENT

.........

IT was tragic seeing a man fall apart the way he did. In every sense of falling—him pirouetting above the school and the tightrope walk across the edge of roofing. And each student and teacher, like hundreds of fingers, pointing and all saying something like *jump*.

I remember his classroom as this very living artifact. Historic antiques of what he thought was American Social Studies—something strictly and undeniably American, like jazz and the Black American, the Black Experience, the transitional process from Africa, to slavery, to freedom— his America when given the chance to narrate history. African tribal masks, pictures of Malcolm and Martin, a replica of the Proclamation, signs "For coloreds only," Jim Crow, Mancala, Paul Collins's "Harriet Tubman's Underground Railroad," and Richard Downey himself, somewhere between telling history and taking on history, as if making quantum leaps into bodies and tongues and stories only footnoted in textbooks. So when walking by his classroom once, I overheard him recite a Frederick

Douglass speech, it gave him this new restorative quality, a flash of life—*Fellow citizens, pardon me, and allow me to ask, why am I called upon to speak here today?* He trotted around the room, speaking to each student, giving him or her his undivided attention, looking from pupil to pupil, trying to reach inside their minds. It was fascinating.

And yet, he slept during department meetings. *Richard, Richard, Richard* one of us was delegated to say, and each *Richard* became more assertive until his shiny bald brown head languorously wiggled, like a turtle, briefly and attentively, and then back into its shell of a suit collar. There was exhaustion in the other teachers' faces that had been brimming for years. This was only my second year. Everyone else pushing twenty years and over—those who worked with Richard their entire career—their frustrations were always moments away from exploding. Once Richard left the room, the babbling critics let loose. *He should retire. He doesn't even teach. He slept through the whole meeting. The kids don't learn.*

I never defended him. But, why should I? He was a bad teacher—forgetful, unorganized, stubborn, temperamental, negligent, subjective—and often hateful to students he did not like. So, it was all justifiable, maybe everything they said was deserved, maybe Richard Downey really was the big problem with education. And even so, even if he was a disservice to hundreds of students' learning, I still felt some civil responsibility for the man.

I'd like to think I was compassionate because it's the right thing to do, like holding the door or helping people with groceries. There's just this certain level of respect for elders, and Richard pushed into his late sixties. Yet, my empathy was rooted somewhere deeper. Richard and I were the only men of color in the entire school—the only Black men in this community within a community; and in this way, I felt accountable. His behavior reflected on me. And in the same way, I felt an unwritten bond of brotherhood with Richard. This created an expectation from the staff and students and even from myself that Richard and I were in constant comparison, juxtaposition, like I was back at the dance-off in high school: *You don't act Black like him. I even forget you're Black. You actually worked hard for your job, and his was Affirmative Action.*

Richard and I didn't speak to each other much. We were mostly passersby in the hallway or faculty lounge. I always tried to be neutral. *Good morning, Richard. Enjoy your day, Richard.* I was always polite and welcoming and so was he. But I think my politeness was subconscious guilt because they say that silence is just as dangerous as insult, and there I was, pardoning for indifference, a bystander to the same mob mentality of ridicule, the very same thing us teachers were trying to teach students how not to be.

But I didn't know what to believe about Richard. I had heard so many stories. It becomes a problem when we narrate other peoples' lives; there's a misconception of what we think we know and the very real story of someone's actual life. The Richard Downey story goes like this: the only reason he earned a teaching degree was because of a free Black scholarship; he was a terrible third grade teacher, but instead of firing him, they sent him to middle school; he taught three different subjects and was equally bad at each;

he was one of the highest paid teachers; he wasn't even a teacher. *He's crazy, Black old fool, never fired because being Black, only hired because being Black. We think we saw him once roaming the streets. We think we know him. We write his story. We watch him fall.*

Richard might have been handsome when he was younger. He had a proclivity for dressing well: iron-pressed pants, straight-pointed collar shirts, ties, suspenders, and single-breasted jackets. For being sixty-three years old, his body was obsidian rock and very soldierly, walking chest first, head high, and back taut. But if you looked at Richard—really sat and touched eyes with the man—you could tell something wasn't right. There was this absence inside of him, like he was never really there. His deterioration wasn't the breakdown of muscle and bone. No, it was intimate, the mind leaving the body, just a constant tremble, like being shut on and off.

.........

Students are wolves to weakness. They watch teachers more than teachers watch them. Students know what they can get away with, they're exploitative and manipulative; they could feel Richard's slow death, and they took full advantage of his decay.

I don't blame them. I did the same thing as a kid. We used to collect straws from milk boxes to use as artillery rifles to defend ourselves against lectures. I ripped pieces of paper and put them in my mouth. Then, like a ramrod, I used mechanical pencil lead to stuff the plastic-straw muzzle with soggy notebook-paper ammo, which I unloaded on the bloated backs of teachers—the little wet globs of spit and old quiz scraps, how our teachers never knew, how we felt like rebels getting back at the educational monarchy. Our Lyme-diseased music teacher didn't know the difference between our claps and our well-orchestrated mouth-farts. She'd sing along—we'd fart even louder. I remember being cruel.

Yes, as cruel as we were, we responded to incompetent authority, and Richard was incompetent. Why not fire him? Why not encourage retirement? Where is the authority above the authority? Where was the accountability? Maybe the administration problem-solved by avoiding the problem. Maybe it took more work to reprimand Richard than to just let him continue teaching. Who really knows what was happening behind the scenes. It's not really my place to say. Though it is easier to point fingers up, rather than back at ourselves. Or maybe, Richard's career was inseparable from his race, hired because being Black and not fired because being Black. They said that every principal wouldn't touch the stove top of race. They hovered around the burner. Firing him would have put the faculty minority male population at zero, so maybe that's why they hired me.

Richard and I taught the same students. While I taught English, I also became their confidant—and not really by choice. Students vented every day, and I tried to channel their frustrations rather than invalidate them. *Mr. Downey has been calling me the wrong name for three months. Our last test had all the answers still circled. He talks to himself in class. He falls asleep during videos. We haven't learned anything past 1865.* I was uncomfortable because I was deeply torn between role-modeling compassion and under-standing and also being in complete agreement with stu-dents' concerns and Richard's lack of teaching. He did talk to himself. He never called me by name. The kids never seemed to be learning anything but Black History.

Students retaliated. Our class conversations turned from concern and frustration to vengeance and malevo-lence. Every instance started the same: *Guess what hap-pened to Mr. Downey today?* And those students who confessed weren't the students committing the pranks; it was the students who felt guilty for what they witnessed. Students would move things around in his room, like his historical figurines or dry-erase markers. They'd put things in drawers, on top of cabinets, or under desks. Students would get his attention while another ran to the projector and shut it off. He'd lecture and then realize the screen was blank. He'd walk back to the computer and turn the pro-jector on. They'd keep this up, until he'd curse at the com-puter—heavy and above his breath. Sometimes he'd just stop teaching and sit at his desk, staring blankly, his eyes just rolling and looking for a way out. And at the end of the day, I would see Richard prowl around the room, mum-bling, searching, slamming, and defeated.

If any students were reprimanded, it was a lunch deten-tion or an after-school detention. But nothing was really being done. And it seemed everyone knew; it was the talk of the faculty lounge and the hallways. Richard was never reprimanded either. He was failing the education system as much as the education system was failing him.

Sometimes Richard used the boys' bathroom instead of the one in the faculty lounge, just because it was closer to his classroom. Male students would joke that they saw Mr. Downey using the urinal, but I never thought anything of it. No one did. And you'd see the man in a six-piece suit waltz out and shake his hands dry.

*Teachers are not to use student lavatories*—we received an email. We then had a grade-level meeting to further discuss the issue: a student had photographed a teacher urinating in a stall. The student snapped the photo on his phone and speculation was that he posted the picture online. Maybe ten minutes later, the boy realized the severity of the prank and deleted the photo. Rumor was, the photo was screenshotted and mass messaged. The boy's parents were contacted, and a further investigation ensued.

We all knew they were talking about Richard, and he had no idea what had happened. During the meeting, he just trembled and nodded his head. In that moment, I didn't know what I wanted to do. I could have cried. I could have screamed at everyone in the room that half smiled like this man wasn't dying alive right in front of us. Maybe I could have saved him with a hug, with some resuscitative measure—something humane and sincere. I could have balled my fist and yelled *my brother!* and stood with him, our brown skin together in testament. I could have told him I loved him, because maybe no one else had said it. I could have said I was sorry. And I was so sorry then, and I still am.

Part of me, besides being regretful, was also scared of Richard—scared of how tragic and yet real his story felt, how far and yet still intimate his tale was, how I could be

the token Black guy, and one day I would experience the
same effects of old age—the degradation of workmanship,
ineffectively educating, losing myself to whatever the world
has thrown and will throw at me—that I could not only replace him but also become Richard.

·········

Richard put in for his retirement that year. He spent the
remaining months of school packing his antiques. After the
bells rang and students left and custodians cleaned, I'd see
him walking from classroom to car, carrying boxes—his
silhouette eclipsing and escaping above the hallway lock-
ers, almost as if it were weeping, as if a ghost. And no one
threw him a retirement party, gave him a card, or even
asked the man *what's next Richard?* Rather, he was dried
and dusted.

Not long after he left, I saw Richard walking along
a busy highway. I beeped and gestured with my hand. I
wanted to stop and give him a ride. He was carrying handfuls of plastic bags filled with groceries. I wanted to help,
but the way he stared—his deep lost eyes looking at me as
if I were someone new, like he was seeing me for the first
time. And there, his nerves might have been pulleys, tugging at each other, trying to drag meaning and make sense,
but there was really nothing left in the man, so he continued, like I never even existed.

# THANKS AND ACKNOWLEDGMENTS

.........

MANY essays featured in this collection have been previously published in literary magazines and journals, sometimes in different form, including: "On I-85 South" (as "Frontier Mother"), *JMWW Journal*, 2020; "My Mother's Mother," *Split Lip Magazine*, 2017, and *A Harp in the Stars: An Anthology of Lyric Essays*, edited by Randon Billings Noble (University of Nebraska Press, 2021); "Bath Time," *Across the Margin*, 2016; "The Reconstruction of a Slave" (as "A Reconstruction of Great Great Grandfather"), *Connotation Press: An Online Artifact*, 2015; "Like Gladiators," *Tahoma Literary Review*, 2016; "Alabama Fire Ants," *Portland Review*, 2014; "Patricide and Boot Shines," *Duende Literary Journal*, 2014; "With My Dad" (as "On Some Things I Wish We Did"), *Word Riot*, November 2015; "Weekend Weather," *Apeiron Review*, February 2016; "O.J. and the Wax Museum," *Barren Magazine*, 2020; "Steve Urkel, Kick the Ball" (as "When Steve Urkel Played

Soccer"), *CRAFT Literary*, 2020; "But I Am Not Toby," *Vagabond City*, 2016; "Angles of the Paint" (as "AND1"), *(b)OINK Zine*, September 2017; "Suicide on the Triples," *Voyage Journal*, 2020; "Shopping with Kris," *Harpoon Review*, 2015; "The Jumps," *Apiary Magazine*, 2019; "5-Series BMW," *Word Riot*, November 2015; "Morning Noise," *Across the Margin*, 2016; "After-School Basketball Game," *trampset Journal*, 2020; "The Best Dancer" (As "Breakdancing Shaped Who I Am As a Black Man and Father"), *Catapult Magazine*, 2021; "The Makings of a Gym Rat," *Drunk Monkeys*, 2020; "In-Between Sirens," *X-R-A-Y Magazine*, 2020; "A Small Lesson on Loitering," *PANK Magazine*, 2020; "On the Confederate Flag," *Ploughshares* Blog, 2020; and "Retirement," *East Jasmine Review*, 2016 and *Porcupine Literary*, 2021. To these literary magazines and journals, thank you.

This collection would not be possible without my wife, who has supported all of my writing. Even during the busiest times of our lives, from graduate school, matrimony, homeownership, and welcoming our daughter and son—through all of that, she has valued my role, not just as her husband and the father of our children but as a storyteller whose voice matters in a community outside of our family. For that, Jennie, I am forever grateful.

Thank you, Mom. You have been an orator of our family history. In many ways, you are as much as the narrator in this collection as I am. Mom, you've always inspired me to just be a good person, to care for people, to listen to them, to find our similarities rather than our differences. Through these essays, Mom, I hope I made you proud.

This book was given a second chance in a world where books are often not given second chances. West Virginia University Press took a chance on *The In-Betweens*. Thank you, Sarah Munroe, marketing manager and acquisitions editor, and WVUP director, Derek Krissoff, for believing in this collection and giving it a new home.

Kate Sherlock, my unofficial lawyer-literary agent and industrious sister-in-law, thank you for your legal advice and fighting for my book.

Initially, *The In-Betweens* was my thesis while completing my master of fine arts in creative writing at Rutgers University–Camden. All of my professors at Rutgers University–Camden played a role in the development of these essays, especially my thesis advisor and friend, Paul Lisicky. Thank you for your guidance, Paul. Your mentorship breathes through every essay written here.

Thank you to the following editors, and specifically to Steve Burns, Chris Campanioni, Ellen Duffer, Amy Eaton, Hannah Grieco, Yi Shun Lai, Randon Billings Noble, Amy Rossi, Arriel Vinson, and many others.

Big thanks to my friend, Tim Hassall, who has been one of the biggest champions. Tim, you told me long ago to never to give up on my writing, no matter how much life will push and pull me, how much life will demand that I stop writing—that in life, there would be no margins for storytelling. But here I am, compiling my acknowledgments. Tim, you said that one day my writing would be in the *New York Times*. While that has not happened, with your encouragement, I believe the *New York Times* is in my future.

The essay "My Mother's Mother" was written about my maternal grandmother, Rosie Jones. Shortly before publishing this collection, my mother's mother passed away. There is real danger when taking on someone else's narrative, as if taking on their body, becoming them, and I hope that I told your story with love and conviction.

To my friends and family—to all the bodies that became this memoir, thank you, and this is for you.